CW00383121

I thank you my families, my

many othcrs, for giving

opportunity to write wιτn
pleasure my true

autobiography

** I Was An Alien **

by

Giuliano Laffranchi

Introduction

I first wrote my own and very personal autobiography some years ago for my lovely families, then of course, penned, polished and self published I realized that none of them were interested of reading it, luckily I only printed 25 copies. Years later my ten years old granddaughter Amy noticed the book on one of my dusty shelves and she asked me; "Can I read it Granddad?" Goodness me I was over the moon, I thought at last I have someone interested in my past. Yes, she read it and she even took it to her school, she kept it amongst her learning books, no doubt she showed it to some of her school friends with some pride. To this day she hasn't said much except she liked it very much, and asked me; "I wish I could write my own autobiography too, will you help me granddad?" I told her that her life story was too short to write, She thought I was right. Regarding my own, she didn't like me mentioning a couple of old flames with their photos in it, naturally I found nothing wrong in that, as these particular flames existed long before I met my wife, but my Amy insisted that there was and there's only one girl in my life and that is her lovely Nan Edie.

I have now reached the year of 2020....I have decided to rewrite it again, what with the atrocious situation we are in, what else is there to do? I can wash my car, cut the grass in the garden, cook a lot of pasta sauces for my famished lot, and then.? Well....we all know we are going through a terrible phase of some kind of a pandemic, they call it Corona Virus. This has taken the whole world by surprise, we cannot go out anywhere as it is very contagious, so we all have to sit in and hope that everything will be back to normal by the time I finish this book, I can only wish that someone out there will find a solution, I sincerely hope it's not the end of the world.... life is too short as it is. In the meantime let me enjoy my memories.

That's me age 9, my very first photo)

Chapter 1

I was born in 1938

Yes, that was a the terrible year, the second world war was just about to shaping up for the worse. I was born, in a small town called Bedizzole, in the Brescia province, not very far from the shores of beautiful Lake Garda, North of Italy. this lake is one of the most fascinating lakes in Europe, its climate is so mite that all around the lake people grow oranges and lemons, for the simple reason that the lake is surrounded by hills and mountains, which prevents cold winds from the East to ruin their growths. Fruits and grapes are the main produce in the region and naturally Lake Garda produces the finest wines, such as the Soave, Lugana, Bardolino, Amarone, Valpolicella, Recioto and many others. Oh..,., I nearly forgot, I arrived the 20th of May, of that year, it was a Friday according to my calculations. I come from a very humble family. My parents never had some of the luxuries we share now days, after the hardship of two world wars, although quite distant from each other, poverty never seemed to disappear from their life. I just about remember the last war, as I came to this world. Hitler had already invaded Austria in the beginning of that year, my father was working on the railways laying tracks during the day and in the evening playing his accordion in various Osteria......(this equals to English pubs), he was earning more money by playing in the evening that working on his day job. He was a very talented man in musical terms, he couldn't read music but he had the perfect pitch, this is a gift by mother nature, not many musicians have it. He was the only bread winner, wages were very low then, we had a Royal family that only fend for themselves and Mussolini who dictated.

Italy with such atrocity that nobody would dare to say a word against him, that was fascism and the black shirts were everywhere with the long baton making sure you did as they said and not as they did. Mussolini was in charge, he spent money he didn't have, I presume he wanted to become another Julius Caesar, his aim was, to conquer Africa and leave us with no food and no jobs and to topple he later associated with Hitler I just about remember, must have been 1944 when the German soldiers, used to knock on our door for some bread, no laugh we were starving ourselves. Then of course a year before the war ended Mussolini was ousted from his power and arrested. Hitler freed him and told him to reform a new Republic, called the Republic of Salo' only ten miles from my town, very easy for him as he chose to live in Gargnano with his young bird Claretta, after leaving his dear wife. Sadly that didn't lasted as they were both caught as they were escaping to Switzerland and killed by the partisans. Their bodies were taken back to Milan and hanged upside down in the main square.

April 1945, just about towards the end of the war, my father was extremely lucky to get a job as a school caretaker, things were improving a bit with steady wages coming in each end of the month, but that wasn't enough to feed three kids, so my father had to carry on to playing his accordion again for a few extra lira, this time he had a partner and that was my brother Pierino he was good playing the comb with his mouth and going around with the a small plate to collect donations, of course, I always wanted to be with them as I loved to listen to their music.

One evening during dinner time my mother, a very tiny beautiful lady always full of ideas of wanting to create something, she suggested that we could open an ice cream parlour in the back room of our house, for this to happen my parents had to apply for a licence to the local council which was granted six months later, only a licence for soft drinks and beer too. Problems started, the ice cream that she made would only last a couple of hours and then melt, naturally her recipe' was not right, she persisted for a few weeks, until she found the right one which became the best ice cream in town, the word spread so quick we started to get so busy that we kept running out of ice cream, of course, because it was made by hand and it took a couple of hours to make three or four kilo that wasn't enough to make our customers happy, luckily later on we found a supplier, which could be added to our home made.

July 1949, I was eleven when I left school, if you wanted to carry on to the secondary you had to pay, my parents could not afford it plus you had to travel to the next big town, I would have liked to, but I understood the problem. So my mother had another bright idea, she ask me what I wanted to do with my life, in other words she wanted to know what kind of profession would I be interested on doing, I honestly was a bit confused at that age, just gone past eleven, my god I hardly travelled to the next town.

So I told my mum that I had no idea what I wanted to do, but I told her that I did like music, and would have like to learn to play an instrument as I already had the taste of it. Yes, in the school where my father worked there was an harmonium, which is it's something like a piano but to play it you have to press the pedals up and down continuously, it was lovely, I used to spent hours in that room pla6ying it, when the school was closed, I could play some tunes with no problems, by ear of course. I wished I never mentioned that! My mother told me that musicians are a lot of drunken sods and she told me; Just look at your father when he goes out playing he comes back drunk. I told her that wasn't his fault as people kept offering him wine to compensate his lovely playing. She wouldn't have it and she suggested that I should learn to be a tailor, for the good reason that whatever the weather, snow, rain or wind I would well under cover and earn some good money because people will always need to dress up... Therefore the best tailor in town took me on, he had about seven or eight people working for him, no kidding, and in no time my boss thought the world of me as I picked up the trade quickly, I was there for roughly eighteen months, I was doing so well, that I could make my own trousers, but he was paying me near enough nothing, although sometimes his wife fed me, she could see I needed nourishment, I was so skinny, I reckoned some strong wing would take me away, I must admit they treat me like one of the family, probably because they only had a daughter and I think they would have liked more kids, but something went wrong to the wife at their daughter's birth. Their daughter was a bit younger than me but on a Sunday she always ask her parent to let me stay for lunch, of course I worked six and a half days a week, we had lunch at twelve and then we would go to the pictures together in the afternoon, sometimes the father came too, but not always. My pay for the week was one hundred lira, which even then I could only buy a bag of sweets and a ticket for the cinema. I was getting a bit depressed, I could see that... yes, I was learning a trade but I was getting nothing in my pocket.

One evening I was having my dinner, actually I was always eating after my family had theirs, because I always got home later, my mother could see that I was not very happy, naturally she started asking me what was wrong. I explained to her that I was not happy in my job as I did not seem to get any money, the pay I was getting it was peanuts perhaps I was too eager at that age, but I never had a cent in my pocket, I couldn't even buy a comic, I couldn't even pay for my haircut, as I had to ask my father to pay the barber for me. She told me to be patient and said that she would

have a word with my boss. On the other hand my father told her that nobody should work for no pay, he considered that slavery. Even me at the age I was, I thought he was right, and that gave me more incentive to work for someone and be compensated, I was determined to do what I thought was right for my future.

Few days later my mother paid a visit to my boss, I was there sawing as usual and all of a sudden I heard my bosses' wife shouting, that he had a visit from Giuliano's mother wishing to have a word, as we were working upstairs on the first floor. Yes, I thought that she came to ask him about my pay, I was pretty sure that I would get something more than a miserable one hundred lira. Fifteen minutes later my boss returned upstairs but didn't say nothing to me, but I heard the full story when I went home for lunch. Well... it wasn't good news at all, but instead I was praised for my good work, he told her that I had a great future in tailoring, as everybody wanted to wear man made suits, I was a fast learner, in fact I was already making my own trousers, but I was not ready to get a full pay, as I was very young, you can imagine I was just gone twelve years old. My mother told me to be patient, everything will be alright in a few years time, feeling very disappointed, I thought, "Ah well... I have no choice but to carry on!" My mum was quite pleased that I was carrying on, but my father wasn't, as once again he said that nobody should work for nothing, and that was that, funny though the next few days my boss never mention anything to me about my mother's visit, I was quite sure that he didn't like that, perhaps he thought he was doing me a favour, considering I was also a babysitter for their daughter Adriana, what a lovely girl she was, few years younger than me, and I could see that she liked me a lot, as we became real young kids an innocent friendship.

I must say a few words about the people I was working with, they certainly were very nice to me and they were my teachers, I learned so much through their expertise that, as I said before I was already making my own trousers, years later I met a cousin of mine, whose one of her daughters was working with me, she told me that they all thought I was a genius with the needle and cotton, good old cousin of mine she's over ninety now.

Chapter 2
My second new job

One Sunday while I was walking home I bumped in a school mate of mine, nice fellow, Ettore was his name, who I had not seen for quite some time, reason was that he was working in a first class restaurant in Brescia town

(The Restaurant where I started a new career, kitchen-porter*)

To my great surprise he was telling me that he washed dishes and pans for four days a week, the other two days doing errands for the restaurant and Sunday off all day, he was getting food and lodgings and three to four thousand lira a month, I suppose with that much money you could buy then quite few things, as my father was earning only ten thousand a month as a school caretaker. I was flabbergasted, he was almost earning as much as my father as he added that he was getting some tips from the waiters too, taking in consideration food and lodgings. I thought for a moment my mate was taking me for a ride, no, he wasn't, he was telling me the truth plus he said that; if he would find someone else to take his place, he would be promoted as a commis waiter, which is more or less working in the restaurant assisting the waiter, laying and clearing tables. I didn't hesitate and said wouldn't mind to take his job, that's was okay by him, he actually seemed happy, he told me to meet him the next day at a bus stop, and go with him, he would introduce me to his boss. Of course I told him about my job with the tailor, how the situation was, not that it matter so much, but I had to have a word with my parents first, I'm sure they would agree and that was an opportunity that I could not miss. I thanked him and said that I would see him at the bus stop the next day without fail.

My parents seemed to decline me to accept such job, as I was too young to work in a big town like Brescia, but after a fierce battle, my mother said she would coming with me and see for herself the place I was going to work and of course the living accommodation. I just couldn't wait for the next day to arrive, I reckon I hardly slept that night.

Monday morning my mother and I met my friend Ettore, of course he wasn't a stranger to her, she knew him well, he was actually pleased to see me and he seemed to be pleased that my mother was coming too. Within an hour we arrived at the famous Ristorante Gambero. We were introduced to my next boss and the job he offered it was exactly what my friend told me, except on little problem, they could not give me lodgings for another couple of weeks, so I had to find my own. Luckily not very far from the restaurant I had my aunt Gigi living in a flat, my mother suggested we could asked her if she would put me up for a couple of weeks. She was more than please to help, but she wasn't very happy about my job as I was only thirteen, then of course I had to walk back to her flat at ten o/clock at night, she was a bit concerned. I started to cry because I wanted that job so much, I told her that I was really bored to sit and sawing at the tailor for nothing. My aunt finally gave in and my mother... well, I think she was pleased too, as there was one less mouth to feed in the family, times were quite hard, but I knew I was facing a new challenge, and not a very easy one. We walk back to my new boss and told him I had my digs for the next few weeks. He was quite happy about that and said I could start the next few days. Went back to Aunt Gigi who gave us a bit of lunch that day, and by afternoon we were back home, getting a few things ready for my small suitcase, as the next day I was going to my aunt to settle in get ready to start my new job the following day.

On my first day I reported at seven am, Luigi the chef was already there and showing me to get the big wood burning cooker going, it took over half an hour to get it in full swing, I particularly didn't like that job, but it had to done, thank god after that I sat down to have my breakfast, a large bowl of caffelatte where I sunk down three large bread rolls in it. After breakfast I was helping the chef to do various jobs, like peeling potatoes washing vegetables, and cleaning around, we all had our lunch eleven am, as at twelve midday the customers started to arrive, and hundreds of crockery and cutlery started to pile in the washer up area, of course on my first day my friend Ettore was showing me how to do it , rubber gloves did not exist then, neither washing up liquid, everything had to be washed up with caustic soda, at the end of the shift my hands where like small pox type hands, I started to get worried but my friend told me not to worry because an hour later they'll be back to normal. Back at six pm, had my dinner and from seven to ten pm the dirty dishes never stop to arrive, thank god by ten thirty the day was over, I realized then that my job wasn't as easy as I thought, I didn't know whether I made the right choice. Few days after as I got back to my aunt Gigi she noticed the state of my hands, she started to worry and there and then she rung my father and told him that he should be ashamed to make a child doing such eavy job, she also mentioned to him my hands' problem. The next day my father came to see me, I was right in the middle of washing up dishes, and of course when he saw my hands he started to panic, he told me I didn't have to do that kind job therefore he told me to come back home, I said I would try a few more days and then I would decide what to do. I thought and thought, but in the end I decided to stay and carry on washing up, after all I started to fit in with the workers, and the food was very good, I really loved those plates of spaghetti, and the chef he was nice to me, maybe because I was looking after his dog.

(That's me in my sleeping quarters with Bobby the dog)

Two weeks went by and the owner offer me to sleep on the premises, but it was in a room attached to the restaurant and that was used every evening by gambling cards players, of course, by eleven pm the room was empty and I had to push in my folding bed which now and then collapsed, that wasn't too bad, but the room had no windows and the stunk of cigarettes and cigar made me feel terrible, but when the restaurant was empty I managed to leave the door open. Then there was another problem, as I already mentioned, Luigi the chef had a small dog, its name was Bobby and his landlady would not let him keep it in his bedroom, so he would leave it with me during the night, I didn't mind, in fact it a bit of company to me, during the day he used to keep it in a small shed behind the restaurant, Luigi appreciated that as he loved his Bobby and for this he was looking after me like a brother, giving me the best of food and sometime a few lira, also all the waiters were very nice, as I was doing little jobs for them they used to compensate me with some of their tips, yes I finally started to see some money which had been unknown to me up to now. Oh, I nearly forgot, My sister Irma was twenty two years old then she used to work for a bakery shop, not very far from the restaurant, actually she didn't work in the shop, she was the cleaner and she cook their meals, my mother taught her to that, she was quite good. So, in the afternoon I used to go and see her and feed me with lovely scones, she also used to gave me a few lira too, saying her boss was good to her, I think she was fiddling them when doing their shopping, she made sure to remind me how rich they were, she used to make me laugh, when she used to say to me; they have more money than brains. I used to tell her, to be a little bit more grateful that they gave her a job, but she didn't like to see so much waste with their children, she used to tell me how they were spoiling them, when we were almost on the bread line, perhaps she was right, we could have been like them if my father's family had the misfortune to lose everything when their big farm caught fire, he had to sell off some of his land and some of his horses to pay for the losses. My grand- father was never the same, having gone through such disaster he started to drink that drove him to his death. When my father used to tell me all this, I remember vividly that he had tears in his eyes, he told me more than once that money doesn't grow on trees. Of course having gone through that tragedy my father had to leave school at the age of nine, they found him a job with another farmer, that is to mind the cows while they were out in the fields, of course that wasn't a very hard job and as a payment he was getting wood for the winter's stove, and sometimes a few meals, what a life, three years in school, but in saying that he had a fairly good knowledge of his grammar and a very good calligraphy, and also he taught himself to play the accordion so he could earn a few more lira playing in various Osterias that is equal to the English pubs, unfortunately he could not read music, but nature gave him the perfect pitch and the good memory of learning a song pretty quick and play it in no time at all.

Chapter 3
A Watch that I did not want !

I found my first month as a washer-upper a bit hard but everything in life has its rewards, so, there I was going home for my monthly weekend leave, yes, I was given an extra day off at ythe end of my first month. Saturday and Sunday plus my three thousand lira in my pocket. As I was waiting at the bus stop, a strange man on a push-bike stopped by and showed me under his jacket a dozen new watches, I was quite impressed by such luxury, as I never had a chance of owning one..... Very nice I thought! He asked me if I wanted to buy one, I asked him the price, he replied that, just for me he would give me a special price and that would be only six thousand lira... silly me, I said: That I only had three thousand lira! Okay, he said... that since it was me he didn't mind losing out.....He told me to chose anyone I liked! I saw this particular one which I really liked so much; it was a cowboy holding a pistol with his hand going back and forward and the other hand giving the time plus it had fluorescent numbers, I thought I'll be able to see the time in the dark..... I gave him the money he gave me the watch. Two minutes later I was so sorry, I wanted to change my mind as my parents were waiting for me for my wages. I looked around, I looked left, I looked right but the man seemed to have vanished from the face of the earth, just disappeared, leaving me with a watch that I really did not want, so, there I was left without my first pay. I thought; What am I going to say to my parents? What a disaster!!

I arrived home late afternoon, I was greeted like a hero, mum had my dinner on the table with a little glass of wine, and of course the first question my parents asked me;

How much did you get? then I was showing in the air three fingers, meaning three thousand lira, again they asked me to show them the money, of course I couldn't, I pull up my jumper 'sleeve and pointed the watch....and started crying. To start with I got a smack from my father, but my mother told him to let me be, I think she felt sorry as much as me, however, I thought I got away with it. I finished my dinner and I went out to play football in the road, traffic was almost nil then, I was gaoling, five minutes went by, when a stupid mate of mine, kicked the ball so hard that he got me on my left arm right on top of my new watch, breaking it into a thousand pieces, I thought the end of the world arrived, I started to cry again, my father came out, ask me what was wrong, I showed him the watch, and bang.... he walloped me again and sending me to bed forthwith. I certainly learned my lesson of how to spend my money.

Early Monday morning. `What a weekend, I certainly won't forget that very easy` I said to myself. I was waiting to catch the bus. Yes, and back to work without my watch, I really wanted to show off, and show it to my friends in work, but it was just like a dream, but carried on as usual and said nothing. Six months went by and I was really getting fed up of washing up, I thought my washing up apprenticeship was nearly at the end, I was ready to embark in my next challenge. I was nearly fourteen then, and from the tips I managed to save from them good hearted waiters I went to a clothes shop and bought a white jacket, a pair of black trousers, a couple of white shirts and a bow tie, I didn't have enough money for a pair of new shoes, I thought I use the old ones, that's the only pair I had, they weren't in a very good state, but I thought they might last for a month or two. Brescia is very wellknown for many little bistro and restaurants. So I set off one by one I went in and asked if they needed a waiter, of course they all ask me, have I done it before? Yes! Where do you work? I told everyone the place where I worked but I didn't say I was washing up dishes. After six o seven restaurants. Finally, I found one who gave me the job, a nice little place called Ristorante la Pace, (The Peace Restaurant) I couldn't have found a better peace, I was so happy I didn't even ask how much I would be paid, it was the owner who said he pay me six thousand lira a month with the food, but no lodgings, and of course I was on a week trial... that's fine I told him he won't be disappointed, but I thought to go back to my aunt Gigi to put me up until I found a room somewhere. My aunt was very pleased as she didn't like me to wash up, she even offered me some money, I said no, she was kind enough to let me sleep in her flat.

My first job as a waiter, and very happy to have passed my week test. A couple of months went by, I was doing so well, the chef was an elderly lady, ever so nice, she really made sure to feed me enough, perhaps she was right, I was so skinny I didn't seem to put any weight on . The customers were all workers of all sorts, and they all loved me, as I was very chatty, in fact I was making more tips than my wages. The owner wasn't too bad, sometimes he was a bit grumpy, that wasn't really a problem but one afternoon as I was washing some glasses behind the bar he approached me and told me that I was getting too many tips, therefore he threaten to cut my wages, at first I thought he was joking. Oh no he wasn't... at the end of that week I was due to be paid, Oh yes he did pay me, but instead of six he gave me four, I asked him if he made a mistake, he said no and confirmed why he paid me less, he even added that I was making a fortune in his restaurant, I told him he wasn't being fair, and said I will tell my big brother. He just laughed at me, maybe I shouldn't have said that.

That weekend I went home and I told my brother Pierino, he said don't worry I'll coming with you on Monday and I'll talk to him. Indeed my brother talked to him and he threaten my boss to report him to the union, there was not an organization as such in catering, so by boss throw us out of the restaurant, and that was the end of my second job. I thanked my brother for organizing my bankruptcy, I don't remember but I think that drove me to tears, to think I was earning as much my father, with the tips. There I was once again looking for a job, this time it was different because wasn't living anymore with my aunt Gigi but I had my digs to worry about. It was a small room in the centre of Brescia, the house was owned by a widow, a nice lady in her fifties called Angela, she charge me for higher rent than usual but now and then she gave me a good breakfast before I went to work. Buit now I was without work, I had to tell her what happened at the ristorante la pace, pace, I said it meant peace, if you can call that peace, my boss nearly declare war to my stupid brother. So Angela said; "don't worry my boy, I know there's an agency that recruits waiters for hotel and restaurant, because my cousin is a waiter and he has been using that place." So she gave me the address, the chap who run it told me I had to pay a fee, plus if I gave a little bonus he could get me a job quicker, I didn't know what he meant by that, but he came out clean and said he loved homemade salami, I told him that we kept a couple of pigs at home and my father made salamis. I went back to digs, I told Angela about what the fellow said, she told me that was a normal thing if you wanted a quick employment. I went home that day and I brought him back a couple of long ones, he took them and put them in a large bag under his desk and he told me not to say a word to anybody. Few days after I went back he offered me a job in the best hotel in town, Hotel Vittoria a real five star one, `this is the place for me, I thought ! Great job, money was good and the working hours were not twelve but down to ten a day, with a day off a week. The customers were all high class, as we say crème de la crème, six months went by, as I was walking home a chap stopped me and ask me how long I worked at the Vittoria, I said six months, he told me he was from the catering union and I had to pay him so much a month because they looked after my job, he even showed me a card with his photograph. I told him I had no money with me, next time I will give it to him. Next day I told my headwaiter about this fellow, he started to laugh, and told me that the catering business hasn't got any union, therefore you to tell him when you see him that if he bothers you again, you will report him to the police. So I did, I never saw that bloke again. Sadly I learned that the country was full of corruption, to get a job in hotels and restaurant it wasn't too bad, but for any other jobs you had to have recommendations here and there, you did not need references, if you were not on the right side you never got a job, that happened to my brother, because he believed in a different party. Yes, that was corruption, sadly Italy was a corrupt nation, which in my opinion it still is. The new republic was formed in 1946 and since then the Italian people had well over 65 prime ministers, and when there is a general election they have a list of more than 25 parties, can you imagine the chaos? Anyway, one day I went to see the chef lady at the ristorante la Pace, the owner was there and he smiled at me and asked me where I was working, I told him at the Hotel Vittoria, he was quite impressed, and as we were talking he said, would I fancy to come back and work for him again, I said, that was nice of him to ask me but I was very happy where I was, anyway, he said that if I change my mind to come back and see him, in the meantime, he told me I could go and see the chef in the kitchen. She was so pleased to see me and she told me that everyone missed me and she whispered that also the boss missed me as he changed five waiters in the last six months, they were all good for nothing, so I told her that he offered me to come back, she said that she knew he would say that, I think he felt sorry to have thrown you out, well, I told her that was my silly old brother, who talks too much for nothing. I said bye, bye to her and told her that I would see her again in the near future, also I said thank you and bye, bye to my ex boos, again he told me.. should I change my mind, I said, I'll think about it!

I enjoyed my time at the Vittoria and I learn a lot, I was approaching fifteen, then, I often remember how many personalities I saw and served there, Buster Keaton, Charley Chaplin, and many others including singing stars of the world Opera, as Brescia has the fourth largest theatre in Italy, as its bars were run by the Vittoria management.

I served and washed many coffee cups and glasses there, and that's where I met Max, lovely fellow a couple years older than me, he was born and lived in Brescia, he was telling me how nice it would be if I joined him to work in a hotel, on the Dolomites for the winter season, I thought why not, it will be an experience and then the money was good too. So, with some regrets I left beautiful Hotel Vittoria. Actually I remember well, that I left that job a bit earlier than I was supposed to, but I thought to take a few weeks off before embarking for the winter season with Max. So in the meantime I was helping my father to tide up the school beautiful park and of course to clean the classrooms, so my mother could have a break from those extra chores, it was a big school to look after and my father was the only caretaker. Now days the same school has three caretakers plus some cleaners, it's unbelievable, and on top of it, he was getting paid peanuts, but I suppose he was lucky to have a job in those days. I remember the school had an harmonium that's where I spend most of my free time, playing it, of course I was playing it by hear as I loved music so much, I always wished to learn how to read and write music, but my parents could not afford it, as far as I can remember shopping was always done on the tick, and quite honestly they never could make ends meet...Those were the days!

Chapter 4
The spectacular Grand Hotel

November 1953.... off I went to Madonna di Campiglio (Alt. 1.550 metres) A magnificent town right up the Dolomites, what a beautiful sceneries, and the hotel was beautiful too. Max and I had a lot of fun, we met quite a few local girls, yes, that's when we started to smell their lovely perfumes and appreciate their beautiful smiles. I remember that pretty red haired she kept pestering me wanting to sleigh ride, I didn't particularly wanted to do that, because I was afraid to have a bad fall and break my leg, that's all I want, we used see a lot of injured people, and the truth was that the management told us that if we injure ourselves we

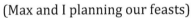
(Max and I planning our feasts)

we were responsible for the costs cost of being hospitalized, in spite of that, Max and I went with a friend of hers, and I did fall a couple of times, thank god I was okay, we took them out for a few drinks a few times, but come six pm we had to go back on duty. Work wasn't all that bad, I was certainly enchanted to see all these rich customers in the evening coming in for dinner in these black suits and tails, of course I was not allowed to serve, all I did is to clear up the plates and the platters with leftovers.

Max and I used nick some of the food, and take up to our bedroom and have a feast, with some vino of course with the compliments of some rich customers. Sometimes when I took the dirty dishes to the washer up area, I used to watch the washers uppers and thought.. was I really doing that? What a job, I must have been crazy to putup with it, but on the other hand someone had to do it. Max was a grade higher than me, he was a wine waiter, he was opening bottles and serve the customers. He was very crafty, he had a hiding place, where he used to put all the wine left over in bottles, and as I said we had our own cellar in our bedroom, it was simply a lot of fun, in fact, I always looked forward to the next working day.

Well.... sadly the winter season came to an end, we really did have a wonderful time, just like a holiday I would say. Max and I parted as he had a job in Switzerland, and I found a job on the Lake Garda, just about ten miles from my little town. It was non the less but the spectacular Grand hotel.

(Me on the Lake - The Grand Hotel in the background)

March 1954 My first summer season on the Lake Garda. The new job was at the massive and luxurious Grand Hotel in Gardone Riviera, it was not only the largest but also a quarter of a mile long a real five stars. I thought I would never get that job, but I did, actually the owner interviewed me I still remember her name Signora Mizzaro, she was quite a lady. She offered me a position as a commis as it was my first year, in saying so the job was good and well rewarded. The owners had also a Hotel on the Dolomites in Sant Martino di Castrozza (Alt. 1,450 metres high up of the Passo Rolle 1,900 alt) Their hotel was called the Sass Maor, also a very big place but enough. So the winter time I was promised a job up the mountains again. I used to love it there, winter time is really beautiful, although full of of snow, you would think that is colder, I don't think that's true, or maybe as I was young I didn't feel the cold as I feel it now.

The season at the Grand Hotel started off beautifully few months later I was promoted Chef de rang, which it means I was in charge of my own station with good satisfactory wages, thanks to this bit of luck I was able to help out my parents, I was earning more than my father did, almost double his wages, it really was a lovely feeling to go home and hand over to my mother more than ever before, I used to remind her that I didn't want to buy a watch, and told she could have the money instead, I remember she had tears in her eyes, they really needed that money, (I seem to have tears in my eyes too as I write this) No matter the feelings, they still wonderful memories, I'm very proud of myself, it's something that I would do all over again. I wonder now days if there are any sixteen years old out there doing that!

The summer at the Grand was over very quickly, a month off and off I went to the dolomites again, this time for three to four months, I enjoyed but I missed my friend Max, he was still in Switzerland, kept in touch now and then by letter. My Dolomite season was over a month off again and back I was again at the Grand Hotel on the Lake for the 1955 summer season. Yes indeed it was a lovely summer. I met a girl she was working in the local pharmacy, we really had a wonderful time, we had a crush on each other, I was seventeen, and she was sixteen, you know that kind of silly first love, she was beautiful, and very intelligent, her name was Orietta, we were carrying on only in secret, she was forbidden by her parents to see me, because I was a waiter, (stuck up lot)mind you I must say that in Italy at that time being a waiter it wasn't one of the best profession, Italian mentality thought it was degrading doing that, and yet many Italian worked in catering for the simple fact that parents could not afford to send their children to secondary schools.

Towards the end of the summer season, (end of October) I thought it would have been nice to change location for my winter season, naturally I was approached by a friend of mine and told me that there was an opening for a chef de rang at one of the best Hotels in Cortina D'Ampezzo, (Alt. 1,231) very famous town as the year before they hosted the winter Olympics. So, without unfairness I approached my kind Lady boss, and I explained that would have like to work somewhere else, and so I explained with a few little lies my ambition to get more good references from another place, she wasn't very happy but she made me promise that I would come back to the Grand for the **1956** season. So there I was in Cortina, what a beautiful town, facing the Mount Cristallo. A five stars Hotel, and I had a good job, I was enjoying my work immensely, There was a group playing every night and became very friendly, they played the sort of music that I liked, and I admired them so much being so good at their age.

I will never forget how well treated was all the staff was at this hotel, the food was superb with your meal you could have a soft drink or a glass of wine, you also had a choice of dessert after your meal, and the bedroom, it was as nice as the customers, every two bedrooms we had a bathroom, mind each bedroom had two beds, but that didn't matter, you'll soon become friends whoever in your bedroom, I remember there was a notice on the inside door, which said; if there was no respect for each other, whoever was, would be dismissed instantly, I can truly say there was more respect than now days. Where ever I worked I don't recall any fights between the staff or anything else. We all seemed to get along nicely, we were just like a big happy family. Although the treatment in that Hotel was one of the best I found, through the season I realized that that boss was very clever, a real businessman. Cortina was not a big town then, but there were enough cafe and restaurants where you could go on your free time, but he, the boss, thought of having a very nice and comfortable large coffee bar for the use of his staff, so the money they earned they would spend it in his premises, his prices were very low, obviously he could afford that, nearly half of the usual price from other coffee bars, he had the music, the gambling machines, and of course food, I thought, it a very good idea, giving from one hand and taking from the other, I have never forgot that system of making money. So as an hotelier he was very clever indeed.

Chapter 5
Switzerland here we come

March 1956. Here I come again to the great Grand Hotel, Orietta and I were still seeing each other, her grand mother was on our side, I remember vividly a particular Sunday I had my day off, and Orietta said to me the day before, that her parents had to go to Milan to see some old relatives, her Nan who was looking after her, thought it was a good idea to meet me and so she suggested to invite me to her house that she would cook us both lunch, I was a bit dubious about the offer, I thought I never had an offer like that before, anyway, I accepted. That Sunday I met Orietta at eleven am, she was so happy to see me, I asked her again if her Nan really wanted to meet me, Orietta assured me that she was cooking some pasta and sausages for us. So there I was, half an hour later meeting her Nan, she was such a lovely lady, not very tall, but quite good looking, I guess she was seventy or more. The lunch was beautiful and so the company, her Nan asked me about my family, she actually knew my little town, as in her younger days she also worked at the Grand, and it was there where she met this chap from my town, she actually told me the name but I forgot it. I thanked her for the lovely lunch, and she actually gave a little kiss on my cheek when she said bye, bye. Orietta and I went for a walk on the lake front and we ended the day by going to the movie. That was a fantastic Sunday considering I was approaching my eighteenth birthday, I felt I went through more years that my actual age, maybe because I started working so young, or perhaps it could have been that I've changed so many jobs and met so many people in that short time, and that helped me to learn a bit more culture than I was taught whether in school or from my parents, I know they tried their best, and

I fully appreciated that as I learned from them the word respect, but you do learn more seeing different places and meeting a lot of different people Past my eighteen birthday I was thinking to learn the French language, a very important number one knowledge in the catering trade, as in that time France was number one in food, wine and hotel service, almost everything in catering. In a letter to Max I asked him a few suggestions of how to get a job in Switzerland, as I had already a good base of French Language. I learned that during my jobs breaks, from a kind Italian teacher working at my father's school, this teacher, born in Italy from French parents spoke perfect French. Max suggested that I should write to a few restaurants in Geneva, very French like in culture and catering. While I was waiting for the right papers including the permit I kept working at the Grand until July. Once I was in possession of the right papers and Passport, good lord I was happy to have one, I kept it under my pillow in case I'd lost it. I quietly knocked on my sweet lady boss's office door and explained the situation of my new venture, actually she was quite pleased and, with her good wishes she told me, she was glad to see me going to learn more about catering and the language adding that maybe one day I would be back at the Grand as a Restaurant Manager, of course, I thank her for all her kindness. And I did apologize for any problems I caused, no one is perfect, but she told me that she prefered someone like who I always said what I thought, than someone who's only talks behind your back. I thought that was nice of her to say that.

My beautiful Orietta was really in tears, maybe we both knew that was the end of our beautiful romance. Although I did write a few letters addressed to the pharmacy where she worked, no way I could write at her address, and she did reply each time, in fact in her last letter she said, although she missed me a lot, she did go to the movie with another boy, so I told her that I would not coming back to the Grand again as my next move would be England, and that was the end of our beautiful relationship. My parents were quite pleased to see me going to Switzerland, because they knew that I was doing something that I liked. My mother gave me a gold chain with a good luck charm which I still wear. I'm sure she had to scrape the barrel to save up for something as expensive as that, but it was a gesture that any of us would keep forever.

August 1956.... There I was on my way to Geneva. Actually I was told that the Swiss didn't like Italians very much, mind you this happens everywhere, I and I thought we'll see. It took me six hours by train to get there, (today's trains only take three hours from where I live) I arrived late at night and of course the restaurant was closed but I was lucky to see someone inside so I knocked on the door, and a gentleman appeared with a lady, you wouldn't believe, it was the owner with his wife getting something I presumed, so he took me upstairs where there was some accommodation for staff and see that I had a bed to sleep for the night, he told me then, that I shall have better accommodation the next day. So far the Swiss people, or him was more than kind. The restaurant was quite big, we were a team of twenty waiters, with a Maitre d'Hotel and an assistant, I was lucky really, I had my lodgings above the restaurant, but that was only provisional, they gave me a couple of months to find a room somewhere else, as these were only kept for the new arrivals. My fellows workers made me really feel welcome, and that's where I met my good friend Dany from Lake Garda, as when he heard I was coming from the region, he came to me and call me "paisa" a very kind gesture of friendliness. From that day we became inseparable, really good mates, especially as we like the same music... and of course the same girls. Six months went by in no time at all, maybe for the reason I was enjoying myself so much, in that time I also started to get some French lesson from an old retired teacher, that really kept me busy. I was determined to learn French. One day something went wrong, well not exactly, but a customer arrived and the maitre was not there neither the assistant, so I sat this chap on a small table as he was on his own, mind you it wasn't the best of the tables, but I thought I put him on my station, usually you prefer having more than one to serve, so you can make more tips, that's the reason I had him, so, no complaints from my mates. The Maitre arrived, he looked at the man and kindly asked him if he was happy sitting at that table, the man replied he was very happy indeed. When the customer went, the Maitre called us lot all together, and I could see that he was livid, that was a bit strange for him to be so upset he seemed to be always very cheerful, but I thought I suppose he had a good reason to like that, after all he had a big responsibility to run a place like this, of course he started shouting and going through us one by one and kept saying why did we put that particular man on that horrible table, I replied that no one was about and thought to serve him myself, nothing wrong I hope, that's it then... it was my fault... so, what was the fuss about? He told me and others that the man was no other.. but Onassis the Greek tycoon. However, we were all on a line, and goodness me what he didn't say, he was really upset and he was looking at me all the time, as if it was entirely my fault, naturally I could not take this lightly any longer, and as I was standing between two doors, one to the lodgings and the other where we kept the brooms and mops, I started shouting back at him, by saying it wasn't my fault. He rightly said; "how you dare to answer me back in that manner?" I replied with tears in my eyes; "I say what I feel to say, it's a free world is it? And grabbed the door handle. (I was determined to go upstairs and get my stuff and leave) But unfortunately I opened the wrong door, and it was the brooms and mops one where all the mops and brooms and the rest fell on me, making everyone laugh, including our Maitre d'hôtel. There I was standing like a Charlie sobbing and flabbergasted, dressed up with mops and brooms around my neck. A week later I was promoted assistant Maitre d'hotel. I wanted to know... Why me? He said; "You are a good worker and you deserve it, I most admire you for taking care of that person than flogging him on to another station, that was a sign of responsibility!

(Promoted as assistant Headwaiter)

Naturally my wages increased and this time I was able to buy myself a real watch, a Swiss watch....Would you believe it? I still have it, it's a Sarcar, very thin 17 rubis, I wouldn't exchange it for an Omega....Oh yes, I would but I would not part with that, even though I don't wear it anymore, I must wear the one my sons gave me for my 60th birthday. Thank you boys!

Chapter 6
Nice to be home again

I was there for nearly a year and it was time to go home for a few weeks rest. My parents were more than please to see me, that was the very first time to be away from home for so many months.

(My mum and dad on the balcony)

Summer 1957... After a short home holiday, there I was back at the old Geneva Airport restaurant, and happy more than ever in my job too, but I was sad to hear that my friend Dany was ready to depart back home, to help his mother to run the small Trattoria in Gargnano, (That is a workers restaurant) he wasn't very pleased, but it was his family that came first, so we had a quick goodbye, and promised to keep in touch, actually we lived only 20 miles apart, that wasn't very far really.

It was a very hot summer day, my friend Giorgio and I had the same a day off, by the way, this friend was from Tuscany he was a bit older than me and he studied at high school to become an accountant, passed all his grades but he could not find a job in Italy, so he ended up to be a waiter

at the Airport, poor old Giorgio he was sad sometime, to think that his parents spent all that money for his high school, and he was telling me that he spent so much time studying and there he was in the same situation as me, nearly I'd say,at least I was assistant to the boss. Somehow, on our day off we spent almost all day long on the shore of Lake Leman, that's the lake in Geneva, not very big, but beautiful, on our way back to the restaurant by bus, actually they still had very old buses, like the pre-war ones, not very comfortable but very cheap to travel, anyway, as we were returning to our working place we saw an advert more like a working class dancing place, yes, we thought we'll have some dinner and pay a visit. We got there, and to our surprise there was no entrance fee, but you have to have a drink. It was quite a pleasant place, nothing to be excited about, but nice. We noticed these two young girls dancing together,   I suggested to go and split them up, Giorgio said I wouldn't there, just watch me, you take the taller I take the smaller, this is a problem I had all my life, being too small, they actually split up with a smile, I think they noticed us and they were waiting for our move, my one was very pretty, the taller one wasn't too bad, but I did fancy the shorter, her name was Vittoria she spoke beautiful French, and when I told I was Italian, she said she was Italian too, but born in France by Italian parents, of course, she did speak good Italian indeed, she also told me that she was working for a very rich family and she was cooking their meals...they had no children. Unlike her friend Elena she was an au-pair, we bought a couple of drinks and we kept dancing, we realized that it was closing time, we walked them home to where they lived, they actually were in the same building in the centre of Geneva, we thank them for the lovely evening, but the worst thing was that we lost the last bus back home so we had to walk, it took us over an hour. The next day I told Giorgio how nice Vittoria was, she was so sweet and gentle and I actually look forward to see her again. He told me that he won't see her friend as he thought that she wasn't interested in him. Well...... Vittoria and I started to see each other a couple of times a week, sometimes she used to come to where I was working, we had some lovely time together. At last I thought, this must be the right girl for me, she used to do my washing, and send it back through the post too sometimes (I don't think many girls would do this now days, indeed most husbands do many house chores, push the baby prams, do the ironing and the washing too.) Vittoria, apart from being pretty she had a heart of gold.

That promotion did me a lot of good, as I was given a couple of weeks off every four months, I was very happy indeed to see my parents more often, so I could take them a little more money than usual, they really missed me, and I missed them too, you can imagine working away since I was twelve years old, sadly this is the hardship of being an immigrant. On this special and particular visit I managed to treat myself to a portable record player, it was a real jewel, I was very jealous of it, nobody could touch it, I started to buy the first 45rpm records, used to be crazy about Pat Boone, The crew cuts singing "Shboom" and fats Domino and naturally the great Frank Sinatra.

Summer 1958. Was almost at the end, autumn went by very fast, but winter seemed to drag on, Geneva is surely cold in the winter, but in spite of all my job was going well, and more than anything I was spending my free time with Vittoria, I was now allowed by the family she worked for, to stay in her room and listen to the radio, she used to go downstairs in the kitchen and she bringing up some food, I asked her if she nicked it, she used to tell me that there so much there, sometimes she had to throw some away, not a bad life, and a few glasses of wine, that part of Swiss they produce some excellent red wine, I used to like the Dole wine, a red classic, actually you didn't see much white then. Spring 1959 was knocking at the door and I was coming up for my 21st birthday, so it was time to plan my next dream; Great Britain. Then you had to be twenty one to be allowed to enter England, and more than anything you had to have a working permit, for no less than one year. So I thought about my good friend Max as I knew the previous year he worked in Guernsey, now he was working in Germany, what a boy he was then. I wrote to him for some guidance, and he was kind enough to send me addresses of hotels and how to apply, so I did and within a couple of weeks I received a working permit from one of the tops hotels in London, The May Fair Hotel right in the centre of London. I gave my notice to Geneva and said bye, bye to all my good friends and naturally a sad goodbye to Vittoria with a promise that she would join me soon, as she wanted to learn English too.

Chapter 7

On my way to Great Britain

1959. Spent the whole of August on the beautiful Lake Garda beaches with my local friends, it was well deserved vacation, and every single day I looked forward for my departure to London.

Preparations were all laid down for me, even bought myself a new suitcase, I still have that, my only possession when I arrived in England. My father who's never been that far, except to Africa during the first world war, warned me to get a taxi as soon as I arrived to London, that way it would make it easier to get to my work destination. The train journey was not very pleasant, I left Milan station at ten the morning and I arrived in Dover around midday the next day, I travel second class, and we were six travelling in a small compartment, I thought, never mind I'll soon be there. Dover station at western docks was massive, before I caught the train to London I was scrutinized by the customs or police, all I know they made me sign some papers and gave me a green booklet called the Alien Order.

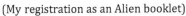

(My registration as an Alien booklet)

So..... there I was an Alien, I always thought that the Aliens were out there in the space, somewhere in the vast galaxy, god knows where. Oh... by the way, in this booklet there is all the Home Office stamped permission for all the jobs that I have change or I've been to first four years, from my arrival. After that I became a sort of resident and now after sixty years of a good residential taxpayer, I was one of the many to be thrown back to my country, because Britain is leaving the EU.... Well, this hasn't happened yet, considering I married a British girl, and my families are all British, I don't really know where I stand now, it is a disgrace, believe me we some plonkers here in England too, getting elected and not doing their job properly. In spite of everything it has been a great adventure, and I must say; taking in consideration the bad and mostly the good, I love Britain.

As I was on my way to London. I certainly wasn't impressed with the train I was travelling on, the Golden Harrow, I still see them wooden seats, the name itself reminded me of the far west, maybe London has some Indian reservations after all, Apache? I shouldn't think so, according to what I read the British Empire is unique, their people is very upper class, and of course I was looking forward to learn from them. As I arrived at Victoria station (London) on the 29th of **August 1959** at four in the afternoon, it was indeed a glorious summer day. I thought I shall have no hassle finding the May Fair Hotel, maybe I could save myself a few pennies if I walk, Max told me that it was near Piccadilly, right in the centre, I walked and walked with my little suitcase, and not knowing the language, two hours later I really felt lost, I finally got a taxi. I arrived at the Hotel ten minutes later and I used the main entrance, silly me, I didn't think they had a staff entrance, there I was in the main reception, showing my papers to the head porter, he arranged for me to sleep in one of the hotel bedrooms, I thought; what a luxury! I was served tea and sandwiches for my dinner, oh, then I had some kind of grass on top of my sandwiches, I was very unsure to eat them or not.

What choice did I have? Of course I had to eat them and drunk my tea with milk for the very first time, in Italy we always served tea with lemon, anyway, better than having to starve until the next day, it wasn't too bad, that was a good sign, meaning that I was getting used to the English way of life. I must have been very tired after that long journey, as it didn't take long before I was dreaming, maybe...... about the Aliens.

Next morning I was taken to the staff Manager, where he took me to my department or restaurant I should say, actually there were four in this hotel; The Chateaubriand, The snack Restaurant, The beachcomber Restaurant, and the Candlelight Room, I was assigned to this last one, this was really a very high class one. Next I was taken to my lodgings, as no member of the staff slept on the premises, believe or not they had a chap in charge just to find lodgings for the hotel staff. I was taken to this old house in Gosfield street, very near Oxfords Circus, I was quite in the centre, and ten minutes walk from the hotel. I was quite disappointed when I entered my bedroom, I had no electricity light, only gas light, there was only one toilette for the whole house, and a little corner sink half way steps up the staircase, the rent was two guineas per week and in advance too. Then this chap took me to Marshall street where he showed me the public baths and then he took me to the police where I had to stamp again my Alien book. and I was told to report once every two months to put my signature on their Alien's book, I presume they wanted to know my movements, I just couldn't believe why we were called Aliens, I didn't even know the meaning of the word, I was a little disappointed, no comparison to Switzerland, I thought England was back in the 1930s. Back to the hotel, just in time for lunch, there I was queuing up with a knife and fork in one hand and a plate on the other with maybe one hundred people in front of me of all races, two Chinese chefs were dishing out some kind of stew with boiled potatoes and peas, some kind of luxury ehh? I wasn't asked to work that lunch but I was told to report for duty at seven in the evening. I was given a free uniform, for a moment I thought I joined the army, I really looked like a soldier from the old Austrian's army, and my duty was as a commis, which meant the lowest grade, my job was to get the food from the kitchen to the restaurant and take the dirty dishes from the restaurant to the washer up area, thank god I wasn't asked to wash up. Each station had one headwaiter, one chef de rang, and me three people for five tables to serve, It had a stage with two bands playing in turn, one was the very famous Harry Roy, playing the oldies and the other it was a Caribbean band Boscoe Holder playing Latin music, he was quite famous too, what a fantastic pianist, later in life he became very famous for his paintings.   The first evening I watched and I was taught how to do my job, I was working with another commis, I was told my training was only for three evenings, then I had to do it on my own, it wasn't really a very hard job, I picked it up the first evening and I was having a good time with the other commis too, he was a nice boy from Ireland, his name was Christopher, we became very good friends, he was lodgings in Maida Vale in a very nice building, his rent was as much as mine, and he had a private bathroom, he was living in this old widow's flat, he told me, but if there's a vacancy he would let me know.

I was talking to some Italians in work and when I told them where I come from, one said there was a chap working as an extra here last night, I think he comes now and then, his name is Max, my goodness that was a surprise, I said to them, I thought he was in Germany, I was told he was working in the city of London only lunch times, says the chap, that's why he was doing some extra work here in the evening. It was a coincidence, I wonder if he'll be back here again soon. Five days later I was at work, when all of a sudden I had a terrible pain in my tummy's right side, I was taken to St George Hospital in Knightsbridge, which was a stone throw from the hotel, and diagnosed appendicitis. The next day they operate on me, putting me out of action for two weeks.   During my stay in hospital I became quite friendly with a young nurse, her name was Julie, she was lovely, she was the one that looked after me, during that time I had a surprise visit from Max and his girls friend, Margaret was her name, and naturally she was German. It was indeed a very nice surprise, they must have told him at the Restaurant, yes, they did, it was wonderful to see Max, I felt like being at home again.

After two weeks in hospital I was sent to Brighton in a nursing home for convalescing for two weeks. It was like a convent, nuns were looking after me very well and the food was quite nice. Few days later I had a phone call from Julie the nurse, she said she had a day off the next day and she would like to come to Brighton to pay me visit, I was astounded, of course I was very pleased, she told me the time she would have arrived, I went to the station, and yes she was there, the only thing that shocked me, was that she was so tall, but so beautiful, I never realized it in the hospital...I wonder if she knew I was much shorter than her? I actually said to her as we were walking; that I never imagine that she was so taller than me, she told me that she didn't mind to be with a smaller fellow. But I thought to myself.... some girls are very particulars about that. (Actually I've been more attracted to tall girls than small ones) However, we had a lovely time on the Brighton beach, I'll say no more.......we enjoyed a bit of lunch together, and she looked so happy...I couldn't believe it. I didn't think it was real, then at five pm I walked her back to the railway station, we said goodbye with a fond embrace...I had to stand on my toes to kiss her. I think she really liked me.... I suppose so, otherwise she wouldn't have come all the way to Brighton to see me.....Sadly I never saw her again, "There goes another sweet dream" I still have some photographs of her which I took on the beach, I think they are in the attic somewhere, my little cheap camera and my transistor radio always followed me wherever I went. Good old companions to keep my memories alive. I still have them.

Chapter 8
Goodbye to Annabella

Back to May Fair Hotel as strong as ever, my fellow workers welcomed me more than I expected, they were so kind they kept my ancient room in Gosfield street, I didn't like it but I put up with it. My work the Candlelight Room was in full swing with Harry Roy and his band, and Boscoe Holder the Caribbean steel band, Boscoe knew I liked music and sometimes he used to pass me the microphone through the back stage from the bamboo canes, so I could sing in Italian without anyone seeing me. The restaurant Manager, used to look on the stage and there was Sam the bass player miming, Gonzi used to say to others; "Doesn't he sings beautiful in Italian?" I was terrible, sometimes I even used to forget the words. I really wasn't very good, but what the hell I thought! What a laugh we used to have, work and pleasure, I loved it every minute.

Few days later I enquired about finding a language school, as my English was almost zero. I managed to find one near my lodgings. It was called LTC London Tuition Centre, I was paying two guineas for four lesson a week, each lesson would last two hours and we were less than ten students in a classroom. My teacher was dressed like a university professor, and spoke better Italian than me. The family where I was staying was Italian, so anything I wanted to know, was easy enough to communicate. They had a seventeen years old daughter, Annabella and by chance she said she could teach me English in the afternoon, when she came home from college, that's wonderful I thought and I insisted that I should pay her, she didn't want to be paid, but I said no I must pay her, her mother she said give her a pound a week, she'd be happy, I was happy too as I was getting tea and biscuits every afternoon. Annabella was very nice and gentle, we became very friendly, one day she asked me if we could go and see a movie together, I told her that her parents might not like that, she said that she would ask them. Permission granted, I always remember the first time we went her father pointed his finger to me and gave me a warning; You behave yourself boy, she's my special little girl! God, I thought if I do something unusual here he might kill me, so I better be good, I remember we used to hold hands like two school children, she kept looking at me and smiling, at me I thought there was something wrong with my face, hope she didn't think I was really an Alien. However, I gave her a couple little pecks on her chicks, in the pictures she used to hold my hand so tight, and leaned her head on my shoulder, I didn't really want that, I felt somehow her father was watching me on my back, I was really a bit scare after his warning, once I said we better be careful, we didn't want the father to see us so close, she told me we didn't do anything wrong as far as she was concerned. Once when we came out of the pictures, she took me to see her college, it was down in South Kensington it was a very old building, she was so proud of her school, in fact she suggested that I picked her up sometimes after school, so I did and the first time she introduce me to her friends, she said I was living in her house and blah, blah... really she wanted to say that I was her boyfriend, but I suppose she couldn't as she knew we were only good mates. She was very intelligent and very grown up for her age, girls usually are more than boys. One day the parents were not in the house, she gave me the usual lesson, and as I left to go up to my bedroom she said to me that she liked me very much, would I kiss her? I said; I didn't want to hurt her but I was thinking to leave as I was going to share a place with friend of mine, so we could save some rent money, she started to cry, she said she didn't want me to leave, she even offered to refuse my pound payment to her, anyway I kissed her and told her that even if I would leave her house I would keep in touch, I would even come to the college, she believed me and that brought back her beautiful smile, but six months were enough for me to go the public baths, a room became available where Christopher was living, so I put together my few things and wait for Christopher he came to give me a hand as I had an extra bag with my suitcase, I said thank you to my landlady and told her to say goodbye to her husband and Annabella, she was still at the college, I don't think she would be very happy not to see me there, but at least she knew that I was leaving the place. We caught a bus and twenty minutes later we arrived at Lanark Mansions we had a room each but we had to share a bathroom, what a beautiful room I had, it was an hotel one, the landlady was very kind, sometimes she even offered us a cup of tea, we had a little kitchenette so we organised ourselves and now and then we used to cook a small dinner, we became friends with a little Chinese chef in work, and for a packet of cigarettes he used to give us a couple of fillet steaks, mind you we took a chance, because if we got searched coming out we would be thrown out of the country, but the food they gave us it was absolutely disgusting, I think it was good enough for pigs. I think I missed Annabella, but on the other hand I didn't want to commit myself any further, mind you I wonder what her father or mother would have said if they found out about our feelings, there were some days that I was very tempted to go and meet her at the college but I always resisted not to... she was too young and I think, I did the right thing. Anyway, the other problem it was Vittoria she was planning to come to England, I think she went to an agency to see if they could find her a job. that's what she said in her last letter from her the day before I moved from Annabella, to Maida Vale so now she had my new address.

Some afternoons I used to go and see my friend Max, he was leaving in Gloucester Place not very far from Oxford street, his place was also nice he had a beautiful room but he had to share a bathroom with a couple of others, Margaret was working nearby, so they were almost together all the time, sometimes he used to cook me a meal, as he was well organised too, he only worked at lunch time and done the occasional extra duty in the evenings at the May Fair and some other restaurants. He was happy to know that I was living in Maida Vale, I was too, but I started to find it quite far from my place of work, and so Christopher too.

One day Christopher told me that he was thinking to change job, without thinking twice he left the Hotel and went to work for a tobacconist in Piccadilly Circus, I was completely shocked. A new job and the owners gave him accommodation too, so there I was left on my own, two weeks later Vittoria arrived, I was very pleased at least I had some company. she found a job as an pair for a wealthy book publisher in South Kensington, she stayed with me for a couple of days before she started work, I took her around London, I could see she was the happiest girl in the world, yes she brought a ray of sunshine in my heart too, she just arrived in time, I don't think she would have liked my young teacher, even though there was no real affectionate attachment on my side, so there she was my Vittoria, only twenty two years old, fresh as a springtime rose. When I picked her up from the railway station I thought I won at the pools, never the less she was my girl. She was very happy with her new job, but a change was happening in her job, the family she was working for had lost their cook, Vittoria told them that she knew how to cook, so they gave her the job and employed another au pair girl. Every weekend her boss and family would leave for their country house, somewhere in the Cotswold, and comeback the following Tuesday morning, I was off every weekend and so I was enjoying my time in that big house with good food and superb wine, my god I lived like a king, she was a bloody good cook if I may say so, we watched television, we used to go for long walks... Oh by the way, this publisher used to have a massive wine cellar, I completely forgot to thank him for his generosity.

Vittoria started to come to the same language school, and she was doing really well, she was better leaner than me, I was a bit jealous about that, she picked up English very easy, she used to say to me, the reason was, she talked a lot with the two children of the household, I didn't believe that, in fact she confessed later that she had few months lessons in Geneva prior her departure to England....

She was so cheeky and crafty, but I loved her, she was extremely good to me, sometimes I was a bit too demanding. After school we used to go for a coffee and a sandwich, she didn't want to eat as she used to tell me, she had so much of it where she was working, after that we used to go and see the a cartoons pictures which lasted only one hour, I used to love that, never watched so many cartoons in my life, she used to love to go to Trafalgar square and feed the pigeons, silly little things but they made us very happy. Who was I to think that at a later stage I became infatuated with another silly girtl, which when I thought afterwards she made my life a misery? Well..... you never know what's going to happen in the future.

Chapter 9
The magic of Mike Mckenzie

One day I came up with the idea of wanting to learn the piano, then one evening I was talking to Sam the bass player and mentioned such idea, he suggested that his brother Mike, who was a professional well known jazz piano player, he would have liked to help me out. So I rung Mike, and to my delight he was willing to give me one lesson a week, for a pound each time. The following week I went to meet him and his family, and at the same time he gave the first lesson, at the end he gave me an address where I could go and practice the piano, for the price of a few shillings.

(The genius Mike Mckenzie at his piano)

I was very willing to learn, but I found it quite difficult to move my fingers in true mode and yet, I discovered that I could create tunes very easy. So, one day I showed Mike some of mine new compositions, he was quite surprised, he suggested that I should try and write some more, but I said it would impossible for me to do that, as I could not write music properly, he suggested that the knowledge of writing was not that important, "As it happens" he said "Irving Berlin the well known American songwriter never could write a single note and yes he wrote more than one thousand hit songs" That's very encouraging, I thought! So I started to write in collaboration with Mike, we wrote together many songs, I was the creator, he was the master, writer, arranger and player and of course singer sometimes, he was really a great artist with the perfect pitch (like my father.) So while I was busy with those sorts of creations, I was also busy with my love life. I never thought I would get in trouble with two girls, but funny enough I did.

I felt somehow lost without Christopher and sheer luck one day I saw Max and he told me that a bedroom was available where he was living, goodness me I thought, in Gloucester Place, I'll be very near the hotel, Max asked me two pounds to give to the landlady to make sure that the room was mine, anyway, a week later I moved in where Max was.

I was so happy with Vittoria that I never realized I would fall for another girl, her name was Elizabeth, she worked in the same hotel as I did, we became very friendly, that kind of friendliness that turned into an affair. I met Elizabeth just before Vittoria arrived in England, to make the situation more perfect between me and Elizabeth she was also living on the corner of the street where i lived, so we also walked home in the eveniong together a couple months went by, I never thought of hurting her Vittoria, so it happened that some afternoons I was a coffee with Elizabeth in this bar very near where I lived, actually in Baker Street, stupid of me, without thinking I used to take Victoria there too now and then. One day Vittoria was looking for me as I was not answering her phone call, by the way, I had a telephone in my bedroom too, that's how nice the place was. Obviously she thought she tries the coffee bar, and there I was with Elizabeth, she didn't say much, there was a very cold introduction, I told Vittoria that I was working with her, but I think she didn't believe me, she was very jealous, the reason I think she did love me too much. She left us and told me to meet her the next day, as she had to go back to south Kensington quickly, she said she had to cook for ten people that evening, and that involved a lot of preparation. Elizabeth was very impressed, she thought she was a nice girl, and she hope she would believe that we were just friends, I told her not to worry, she loves me too much to think that I would go with another girl. Of course I was wrong, I met her the next day, and I thought the world came to an end. Vittoria told me that she already made her decision to go back to Geneva, she would not be a second best of course she said; "Nothing to do with that blond, who ever her name was!" She was lying!" I think she found Elizabeth very attractive and a bit posh the way she talked.I did not want her to go, neither her boss, in fact he rung me up the next day, and pleaded with me to make her stay, he told me that he knew the reason why she was leaving, as Vittoria told her Mrs and they were sorry to lose her as she was so good in everything he asaid, and the children loved her so much. I really understood how he felt, and I told that there was nothing that I could do to prevent this, he told me that he offered her more money, if she stay, but apparently she gave him three weeks the most. The two contenders, that's a laugh, Elizabeth just used me, for all her conveniences, once she obtained what she wanted she couldn't give a toss about anything or anybody else's' problems, I knew she never really wanted me to like sweet Vittoria, there again we all make mistakes in life

Vittoria   *(the two contenders)*   *Elizabeth*

Vittoria didn't come to school for about a week, I didn't think she would taken it so badly, anyway, i wanted to find out, so I kept ringing her, her posh lady used to answer the phone, she was telling me all sorts of lies, such as gone to the pictures, took the children out, just to get me off the hook, she was annoyed because it was my fault for losing her, one Friday I went to her mansion, the family was not there, rung the bell, and there she was opening the door with tears in her eyes, I really felt sorry for her because she really felt hurt. We patched up and that evening she cooked me a nice dinner, we watched the old telly and we talked about our future, keeping the subject light, I kept saying I wanted to learn English properly, before I could make any plans to go back to Switzerland, I didn't want to go back really, if anything we could have done something here in England, she had quite a bit of money in her savings, more than once she told me they belonged to both of us, as for me I didn't have two pennies to rub together she never spent on herself, she used to buy a lot of presents. Monday arrived I had to go back to work, the family would not be back until Tuesday. That afternoon we met at the school, and she gave the bad news, she booked her flight for the following weekend. Her boss would take her to the airport, and he made promise that he wanted to see her back, he also gave her three weeks holidays pay, thinking she would come back, but finally she told that she would not come back,

England was not for her, she did prefer Switzerland, as she thought it was a better country and more safer, after all although she was half Italian , but her mentality was completely Swiss, come to think of her now, I think she was right, she quite intelligent, I could see sometimes that she saw the future better than I. However she told me that If I really loved her I should follow her,. she told me that she was quite fed up to run after me all the time and she added that while she was away, I could have as many coffee as I liked with my blond. I did apologize more than once, and so we went for a coffee, and that seemed she calmed down a bit, goodness me she treated our relation as if we were already married.

Chapter 10
A disappointed visit

September 1960 A year went by and as I ended my contract with the May Fair Hotel, a truly good offer was at the door from my headwaiter, who had left for the Ivy Restaurant, so there I was going to the Ivy too as a chef the rang, but before doing so I asked if I could take a leave for three weeks, that was granted. There was a problem, if I stayed out of England more than two months, I'd have had to have a new permit to enter. In fact you had to be an Alien for four years, after that you were free to come and go as you pleased. Flown to Geneva airport, actually it was a night flight, because they were cheaper then. Vittoria came to meet me, we spent a couple of days together, I found it funny that she had to confess that she met this chap who wanted to marry her so much, but she told me that she was not interested, I wasn't all that interested to those news, I thought maybe she was trying to make jealous, as I was pretty sure that she would never leave me, I simply thought that was a hint, for me to put the famous question "Propose", but there was no way that I could do that...What? right in the middle of my ambition to learn English...No way! Instead I told her that I was going back to London in a couple of weeks, catching the plane from Geneva, and I told her to meet me at Geneva railway station on the date of my return. I Arrived home and my parents were over the moon, stories and happenings were exchanged, and then one day I was alone with my mother, I was quite surprised as she asked me about Vittoria and she said; "Who is this Vittoria then? I keep receiving parcels from Switzerland with chocolates and perfume, is she your girl friend? At that moment I though, she must really love me, what about if she marries the other one? I told my mum that she was just a girl that I was going out with, but there was nothing serious about it, but my mum told me that she must have been very fond of you, to do all that. I told that she was right, and I never realized to that extent, and that was the end of my conversation. During my vacation I visited a lot of relatives and school friends, had a wonderful time, and it was really nice to see my parents so happy, but time was short and I had to leave once more, my mother was in tears and my father...? Well, knew he felt worse than my mother, his eyes were so red as if he had taken drugs, but I reassured them the I would be back soon.

Early morning I caught a train from Brescia to Geneva. I got there around lunch time. I waited for over an hour and no sign of VIttoria, I thought that was very strange, as she never let me down, I went to the place where she was working, and they told she had a day off, I went to her place, I rung and rung the bell, but she would not answer, I knew she was in there as I saw a couple of lights on, well... so I had no other alternative but to set off to the airport which my flight was scheduled at five pm. I was very annoyed as I had a present for her, and more than anything I was truly ready to propose, still I thought I will find out one way or the other. When I got back to London I wrote a long letter. Got an answer, which she said she forgot the date of my return, then she said that maybe that was an excuse, and she admitted that she was with the fellow that day, but she said that nothing had happened, of course I wouldn't have believed that if she had opened the door, also she added that this fellow asked her to marry her as soon as possible. Well.... how's that for luck? What a revenge!! I simply didn't know whether to cry or laugh, I was quite devastated, and very upset as I did not want this to happen, in the end I cared about the girl, but it was too late. What can you do?

You win some, you lose some! I had a few days off before I started my new job, and I past the time with some of my friends I used to work with. They asked about my holiday and the visit to Vittoria, I told themthat we decided to part and choose our own way of life as she wanted to stay in Switzerland and I wanted to stay in England, can you imagine if I told them that she was with another fellow?

They were quite happy to have a nice piece of Parmesan that I brought back from Italy, and was good enough to enjoy a nice plate of pasta in between our music sessions and playing cards. Unlike Max he was rather busy with his girl friend Margaret, but on the side he was not an angel either, he didn't let his secrets out too many times, he was a dark horse, if you know what I mean.

Started my new job. The Ivy made me very welcomed, my headwaiter was pleased and proud to see me, as I did my job right. He put me right in front of the restaurant where the best tables were and best customers. I really met and served many famous people, just to mention a few, Adam Faith, Michael Caine, Marlon Brando and many others. A couple months later I got a job for my friend Franco as usual, our friendship goes back to our Lake Garda times, and where ever I went

I always found a job for him, and that is Switzerland, London and Cornwall. but since he had parted from his wife, divorced her and remarried he became another man, or maybe it was that when you make a few bobs in life, you don't really want to know your old friend. (More of this later) I stayed with the Ivy Restaurant over a year and in November **1962** I join the well known fish Restaurant "The Overton" in St James's street, quite near to the May Fair. I left Franco back at the Ivy, he was quite happy there.

The Overton was as classy as the Ivy, and the reason I left it was because the money was better and I had two days off a week. The restaurant only had fish on their menu, that's where I got the taste of oysters, I used to love them, one day a week I had to do an afternoon duty, to do the hover and to mind the phone, so I finished at seven pm. It was a good job indeed with a lot of free time that for my musical hobby and school, but I suppose I got a little bonus working there. Yes there was this gorgeous young divorcee call Mary, she was looking after the cloakroom, I just don't know how it happened, she kept smiling at me, so I asked her out for coffee one afternoon and she told me all her life story, that her husband left her for a younger model, good lord, Mary was only twenty five, yes he got an eighteen year old bird, so Mary got stuck with a daughter to raise with no daddy. I felt sorry for her. I was introduce to her mother and every Sunday I was invited there for lunch, in the evening Mary and I used to have dinner in my place, living the mother to babysit. The mother was always so inquisitive, asking unwanted questions, such as, "Are you thing of settling down Julian?" Mary knew very well that I had no intention of getting married, and she told me many times not to take any notice of her mum. Of course the other problem was that I wouldn't have dared to take back to my parents a wife with a daughter from another fellow, my parents were Roman Catholics and I suppose a bit old fashioned, and I respected their mentality, nowadays you do whatever you feel, we live in a different world, anything goes now. Anyway, they were different times then. Beginning of summer business was a little bit quiet at Overton, and I think we were over staffed, so we were offered a couple of weeks off with less money, I raised my hand quickly, I thought I could have a London holiday. I started my two weeks break, morning I was going to the piano studios to practice, you can imagine for a couple of shillings I could stay there for four hours, Max was working in the city still so he had the afternoons free, we would spend time visiting museums and walking in the parks, and go to pictures, and in the evening we used to have dinner in our place sharing everything, except the girls of course, sometime his girl friend Margaret used to come, and sometime I had Mary. Two weeks passed too fast and there I was back at the fishy place, I really needed that extra pounds desperately, but in the end money was never an issue for me as I was very careful with it, my motto was, "never borrow, never be penniless" as long as I had a job, I was always a good budgeter.

Chapter 11
Principessa Bimbaneve

One night I dreamt about a little story, a children fairy tale, the next day I wrote it down in Italian, managing to finish it in a couple of days, it was a winter story and called it in Italian "Principessa Bimbaneve" which it mean The "Snowgirl Princess", but in English I thought I call it "Princess Snowdrop" as the snowdrops are the main ingredients of the story, I shelved it and never thought about it, I didn't dare to show it to anyone as I didn't want anybody to laugh about it. By this time my affair with Mary started to fade away. The problem was the little girl, she was ever so nice, I could see that she missing her dad desperately, of course first I was uncle Julian, then she used to say that she wanted a daddy like me, that didn't add up, I didn't want a position like that, again I thought about my parents.

(My first reel to reel tape recorder)

April 1962.   I successfully achieved my Diploma of English from the glorious school London Tuition Centre, I was proud with myself, but I found that, not only me but my professor too that I was much better in writing and spelling than speaking it, however that was quite satisfactory. Let's face it, I will never lose my Italian accent, no matter how much more I will learn it. Well... there you are... so, I thought, I don't have to pay the school anymore, so I will treat myself to a present. It was a reel to reel tape recorder made in Germany, a real luxury then, I bought it in Edward road it was quite expensive 52 guineas, I put down 15 pounds deposit and the rest I was paying two pounds a weeks, but I had to live my passport with the shop as a security, of course to pay it off quickly I was doing another little job, I was getting up at six in the morning to start a seven three times a week to breakfasts, back at the May Fair Chateaubriand restaurant for a pound each morning, it was hard as I was going to bed late at night, but in a couple of months I managed to pay it off and get my passport back.

One evening I said to Max;   "I have written a children story" he smiled at me and said "I hope is better than your songs" I took no offence, because I knew he didn't dislike them that much, however, I show it to him and thought the moral of the story was very good, so I asked him if he could translated for me not the whole story but a short synopsis, as his English was better than mine, on the contrary he said that my English was good too, I translated and wrote the synopsis myself, he corrected a few lines. A few days later I took it to a music publisher, in Bond Street, Mellin Music (That took some courage to take a story just like that, if you do that nowadays they throw it back at you) which I knew already the manager called Len Black, as I did take a few songs there which I wrote with Mike. Len read it, and said that it would pass it on to his boss Robert Mellin, quite a famous chap he wrote songs even for Frank Sinatra.

Few days later Len rung me up and asked me to go and see him, my god my legs went jelly, I went to his office the next day and he plainly told me that Mr Mellin liked the story very much, he thinks that it could be a very good children Musical fairy tale, I was flabbergasted I just couldn't believe it, I said that I had no problems writing songs for it but no way I could do the lyrics for it nor the script. He told that wasn't a problem he said that he would get me the best lyric writer in London. I went back to Mike and his wife, showed them the story and told them what the publisher said, they just couldn't believe it, plus I showed Mike some of the tunes that I already written to be included, we got down to work, Mike put them down on tape and subsequently Len introduced me to Jeff Ryan the lyric writer, we went into a coffee bar showed him the story and gave him the recorded songs, we discussed various plots of the story, he said he would go home and try to do something and see what he could come up with, that left me with a little hope, but I thought I had nothing to lose. Jeff was already a well know figure to the Tin Pan Alley, (That is the centre of the pop music situated in Denmark Street in central London.) as he had already a few songs in the top ten. A week later Jeff rung me up, asking me if we could meet at the same coffee bar. I just couldn't believe it he came up with nine lyrics for the songs and the script, no lies, he really completed the whole job in one week, clever old sod. Jeff has written a lot of stuff including some big musical shows, but his bad temper didn't get him very far, for instance if a pop star would change a line of his lyrics, he would retrieve his song, and yet he always was desperate for money. Poor old Jeff he was always penniless.

Mike was very happy, I was extremely happy, so we arrange to do a recording at Jeff's house, with Mike at the piano and some borrowed singers, plus a special recording machine which Jeff managed to borrow from an engineer from the BBC friend of his, at the end of the day we were all over the moon with the outcome. Few days later we took the recording to the publisher, who gave us an agreement with three advance royalties cheques. The publisher knew exactly what he was doing, in fact he already been in touch with an European film company, for a cartoon feature film, but unfortunately six months later that company went bust, but that wasn't the end of it, Mellin Music kept trying to sell the product to other companies, but years went by without any consolations.

March 1963 I couldn't wait for something that wasn't going to happen, I knew from that disappointment that music business was difficult, so my life carried on as usual, I knew my bread and butter was the catering business unlike my friend Jeff was always waiting for something to happen, in the end he also had to do some various jobs, to feed his habits. I must admit though, I was sad and disappointed, but I understood the situation as I didn't have to depend on it, so I put Princess Snowdrop on a shelf and I thought this can't be the end of my luck, I really thought I needed a change of air. In the meantime Max was organising his life as he was just about to tight the knot with Margaret, good old Max he'll be soon an old married man, I never thought he would become so sensible. So there they were husband and wife, they had been together quite a few years, he met her while working in Germany, the rascal speaks good German too, I think he was fed up to be a bachelor. However he had a very simple wedding, as they needed all the money they could get to set up their flat. They went to live in Bayswater, which is pretty central. Unfortunately I was left on my own, I missed his company, the long chats, the endless hours of music listening, and the long walks, he would never get tired. One Sunday we walked to Heathrow airport and back, didn't actually realized that we walked that far, we got back late at night absolutely knackered.

Chapter 12

A change of air

Franco was now working in a small restaurant in South Kensington, I called him and said that I needed a change of air, as by now Mary and I split up, and naturally now and then I used to see Elizabeth, only when I felt like, she used to call me quite often, but I don't think I ever forgiven her for losing my Vittoria, and she knew that it was her the cause of it.

Franco and I went for a coffee the next day and discussed the change of air, we thought why not try the seaside, Cornwall was the choice, as we were told that beaches were really fabulous. I thought the best way was to go and an agency, so we did, the choice was enormous, we took a chance and chose Newquay. The agent gave us all the details and two weeks later we were at Paddington railway station waiting for the train. As we were quite early, we went into the coffee shop to have a cup of tea, the place was very busy but we managed to get the last table. While sipping our brew and minding our own business two young girls approached our table as we had two free seats, they kindly asked if they could sit on those "Be our guest" I don't think they appreciated that answer, as they didn't smile or even said thank you, perhaps it was our accent or maybe they thought we were Aliens, their accent was also strange, it wasn't a very good English at all, they spoke in very short phrases, we could hardly understand them, I remember I read in a book that some kind of accent like that, could only be **cockney** from London's east end. A total silence fell on our table, while they were sipping their tea I said something to Franco in Italian, like; you take the tall one and I take the small, this is because Franco he's a bit taller than me, and one of the two girls was taller than the other... they looked at me as if I killed someone, I don't think they found it amusing, they quickly drunk their tea and off they went, without even say bye, bye, or thank you for letting us sit here, or something like that. I said to Franco, they could speak Italian too, they must have understood what I said, he said,. Italian... ? Do us a favour, they can hardly speak English, let alone Italian. We could see them walking from the coffee bar walking up and down waiting for the train, but all of a sudden they disappeared. I told Franco that I did fancy the blond one but she was too tall for me, he told me that he didn't like my attitude, if they come back he would sea t at another table, don't worry they won't come back I assured him.. While finishing our tea, we were discussing and wondering what kind of Hotel that agency gave us, let us hope for the best, Franco replied. The journey wasn't all that pleasant, half way we had to change train, I'm not so sure but I think it took us four or five hours to get there, we asked a porter where the hotel St Rumons was, so we could get a taxi, but he said it was nearby about ten minutes walk, as we were walking to the hotel I said to Franco that I was surprised not to see them two girls on the train, I bet they got on a different one, he told me I could be right, he was surprised too.

We got to the hotel, not a very impressive hotel I said. it wasn't opened yet, but someone was at the reception, we gave our papers from the agency, and he said everything was in order, this chap took us to our quarter, they looked like wooden sheds, but inside they were okay, they had what we needed, males on one side and females on the other he told us to come down at six for the dinner, where we also we will get some instructions and meet our headwaiter, the hotel would opening the following weekend.Went down for dinner and as we enter the staff dining room, then there they were the two mysterious and beautiful girls from Paddington Station, we could not believe it, they look at us, we looked at them and the four of us burst out laughing and that broke the ice. We had a lovely introduction Edie was the short and Maureen the taller and I said right away: " I didn't think you enjoyed that tea in Paddington as you quickly disappeared" they both laugh.

We invited them out for drinks that evening, no it wasn't champagne, but we went to a pub to have some beer and crisps to celebrate our lovely meeting, we enjoyed tremendously, as we were back to our rooms, we said what a coincidence, no way that wouldn't happen in a million years. Never the less, the following evening we done the same thing, actually they wanted to pay, I said I didn't want to offend them, but if they insisted... please let me be your guest, they went all serious, and I said I was joking... no they said they wanted to pay, Franco said let them pay, tomorrow night you will pay. I said; thank you mate! It was all a good laugh. As the week went on we took it for granted and it became a habit, we went out every evening, and we started to enjoy a very tenderly friendship, especially on our return to our digs, we used to spend hours chatting rubbish, as long as we made them interested in our well being, goodness know what they saw on us, mind you what did we see on them? Yes, they were beautiful... a lot of other staff envied us. Then a little problem started I was serving a family from Sale, they had a daughter called Kay, she just wouldn't leave me alone, one morning I took their breakfast to their bedroom, and there they were mother and daughter inviting me to seat on the bed with them, I felt so embarrassed that I left the room, I could hear them laughing, At first I thought they were joking, then later in the afternoon by the pool Kay approached me and said sorry, and told me that she loved me, I told her that I had a girlfriend and I thought that was the end, two days later they left the Hotel, Kay came to say bye, bye, she was crying, we had a little embrace and a friendly kiss, she ask me could she keep in touch, I said , yes, so she kept writing to me a few nice letters, but slowly that faded away.

Chapter 13
The great Bedruthan Steps Hotel

We told Edie and Maureen that we didn't like to work at the   St. Rumons, but yet we did not make any planes to look for another place, but we were seriously thinking, they didn't like that, obviously they wanted us to stay, so we promised that if we ever left we wouldn't have gone very far, of course....Their job was quite different than ours, making bed in one place can't be different to make it in another, still for the moment we were enjoying their company, and without a doubt they were enjoying ours.

As we thought they were both from the east end of London, they had been friends since school days. Fed up with the London life they also wanted a change of air, so they became chambermaids at the St. Rumons Hotel, As time went by we became more than friendly too, we used to have some fun down at the beach, almost every afternoon, in the evening after work we used to go out for walks and the usual pint of beer with a packet of crisps, But again St Rumons was not our kind of place, a month later we were offered a job in a bigger Hotel, just outside Newquay, and that was The bedruthan Steps Hotel, for better pay and better conditions naturally.

June 1963 We moved to Bedruthan Steps, what a difference, yes we were much happier, and our girls used to come up almost every evenings it would only take ten minutes by bus from Newquay, or sometimes we used to go down ourselves, because by nine pm or just after we would be finishing our duty. Our boss started to appreciate our expertise in our work and within two months Franco became wine waiter, and I became assistant Restaurant

Manger, or second in charge. The restaurant Manager was Dutch and he simply didn't get on with the boss Peter Whittington, Peter was a nice chap, but if he didn't have his way he could be very argumentative, and so he didn't agree how the restaurant manager was running the joint, I must admit he didn't like him at all, so one day they had an arguments about setting the restaurant for a dinner and dance layout, that was once a week, and it seemed that the argument would not end, I could see my manager couldn't take any more he told him that he had enough of him, and told the boss what to do with his job, the next few hours I saw my Restaurant manager loading up his car and heading for a new job. Incidentally, he had his wife with him and she was pregnant. Yes... you guessed it, I was promoted Restaurant Manager, I probably wasn't earning as much as the Dutch, but my wages went up considerably to mysatisfaction. The job was not very easy, but my Swiss experience help me a lot, what with more than twenty waiters, and over four hundred guest to feed at breakfast, lunch, and dinner, (Nowadays they have two shifts, which it means; their duty work no more than eight hours a day, in the sixty you had to work ten hours a day) So my hours were a few more each day but Edie was quite happy, as I thought she must like me, of course I liked her very much, she was very slim and very pretty, Maureen was pretty too and blond, to begin first I said before I did fancy Maureen, don't know why I always go for taller girls and the tall ones tend to go for me,   (I am lying really.) I think the grass seems to be always greener on the other side.

(Edie and I overlooking the beaches of Bedruthan Steps)

The end of the season was imminent, My Boss called me in the office and told that if I would come back the next season, he would pay me a retainer of five pounds a week for all the weeks the hotel would be closed, but I will be able to collect such retainer only at the end of the following season, if I complete it of course. I thought that was fair enough, I really had nothing to lose, I accepted his offer and I think it was quite fair at the time, when back in London I would get around eighteen pounds a week for a job, and lucky to find one plus I had to pay for my digs. A lot of work was put in to close the hotel for the winter, and because Edie and Maureen finished before us they came to help us, and got paid too I recall. Towards the end I asked Edie if she would come to Italy to meet my parents, when my boss heard that, he said he was planning to go to Italy too by car with his wife Mary, and he would be delighted to meet us up around Lake Garda, as Franco and Maureen decided to do the same thing. We finished at the hotel and we were getting ready to go back to London, and of course I had to face Edie's family, I was really looking forward to see what it was like the east end of London.... I was thinking I heard so many stories about Jack the Ripper....I wonder!

Quite nice lot they were, the Thompson family, a very small lot indeed, real east enders, I had to get used to their accent, as at first they were talking so fast, eating some of the words, but then in time I could understand them, I often wondered what they thought of me. Edic's mother she had a heart of gold, she'd do anything for anybody, she never really went further afar that the east end of London, because the first thing she asked me, it was where I come from, I said to make it easier "Milan" she replied; "Oh that's nice they a lot of sunshine in Spain" Edie then jumped in and told her that Milan was in Italy.

Edie lost her father when she was seven, her mother then remarried as she had two kid to bring up and to feed, life was not easy then, very unlikely to get a juicy benefit from the government like now days, everyone had to work, dole money was very little, thank God I never took a penny from the state in all the years I've been in England, that's quite a record according to what I have seen all these years. been. Ialways considered that a degradation, but a lot of English and foreigners now makes a feast out of it. Her brother Peter a down to hearth fellow, the step father Harry, was very quiet, never talked much about himself. However it was nice to meet them all. A down to hearth family.

Chapter 14
A very enjoyable holiday

After a few days at Edie's house, we departed to Italy, by train of course Franco did the same, he took Maureen to meet his family, then we arranged that we could all meet at my house, including the Whittington's, and by the time he joined us he had already been around half of Italy, Anyway we met at my house and my mother cooked us a special veal recipe, we had a superb and enjoyable meal and wine. Although they were our bosses a real friendship started to grow, no way you could associate with the some Italian Hoteliers in such way, they really considered us part of the family, in fact at their hotel we were treated first class, we lived in proper rooms and we even had our own television lounge, and the food they gave us it was first class.... I must say they were good genial bosses.

In the afternoon we visited my little town and the surrounding of Lake Garda which the thought very beautiful, we took them to Gardone Riviera and we show them the Grand Hotel where we used to work, they found it very impressive, then we visited the Vittoriale which was the residence of the famous Gabriele D'Annunzio, this place was really spectacular. The Whittington's took then to a famous Restaurant when we had the biggest trout I ever seen, it was a memorable day.

Edie and I enjoyed the rest of our holiday with my parents by visiting various places and of course we went to Brescia quite a few times, and Edie had the pleasure to meet my aunt Gigi, a delightful lady, who looked after me at the beginning of my catering adventure.

It was a sad day to leave my parents again, at least they were very pleased to have met Edie they did like her very much, so in a very short time we were back in London. I was staying at Edie's place while I was looking for a temporary job, only for a couple of months. With a bit of

luck I found a job in Ilford not very far from Edie's house and at the same time I became a correspondent for an Italian Music Magazine.

(My reporter pass)

I managed to do a few interview to some pop stars and film stars, I think the best which I shall never forget it was with Marlon Brando, in the restaurant where I was working, what a cheek... the head barman said, Actually I was in charge on that job, it was in Chelsea, very posh place. After I served him the coffee, I said to him that I was also a freelance news reporter for an Italian Music Magazine, apart from being a waiter, he looked at me and he laughed, he was with two other fellows fellow I don't know who they were, but I don't think they looked very pleased! I showed him my Identity card and I also apologized for interrupting his meeting with his two guests, I only asked if he was filming in London, he said very nicely that he was filming with Sofia Loren, he gave me his autograph, and he told me that I was a better reporter than a waiter and added: "Just carry on be a reporter Giuliano" Easy for him to say that, but I did hardly get paid when the magazine published it. Really, all I got for doing this kind of reporting it was simply their weekly magazine free of change, However hat kept me informed about the Italian music situation, I was very much interested then, I used to buy quite a lot of Italian records then, it was always nice to hear or see what was happening in the old country of mine, it does take a long time to get rid of the Italian mentality, That's all gone now, I am eighty five per cent British un-nationalized. Now days you can keep in touch with the television, the satellite that brings everything, naturally you can listen to the radio much easier now, from all over the world, what an incredible technology we have! Aren't this new generation lucky? Possibly they don't know it!

March 1964... Edie and I went down to Bedruthan Steps Cornwall for the new season, I was a Restaurant Manager and Edie was a chambermaid, of course there was no problem to get a job for her, Mary offered her one, when she met her the year before. Franco and Maureen didn't come, they decided to stay in London. We were very happy at the Hotel the Whittington used to let us use on our day off their summer house in Plymouth, which was in the middle of Edgcumbe Park.

I was very happy with my team of waiters and my second David Blaney was a character, then the assistant to the general Manager Eugene was a fantastic fellow, we really had some fun the three of us. I became very friendly with the band which now and then they used to play my songs, and one evening the general manager suggested that we should have a talent contest, Eugene was a good singer too, I didn't want to participate I was sort of pushed in, anyway I sang a song of mine "You gotta kiss me goodnight" and Eugene sung "I left my heart in San Francisco" we both got to the final, and funny enough I won, but I must admit Eugene was better that me... well, the first price it was a little silver cup, that you can hardly see it, but it's nice, I still have it on one of my shelves. It was very exciting...What.... with four hundred people watching? I'd say so.

This must the smallest winner cup in the world, I think I should go in the Guinness book of records.

Chapter 15
A glorious football team

It was a very hot July, and that was the day after that magnificent talent contest, which I will not mention again. Just finished my breakfast, when out of the blue, I had a phone call, it was Elizabeth, she was staying in a small guest house in Newquay, in the company of her friend, I even remember her name, Helen that's alright, very pretty girl too. She said they were at they were at my hotel the previous evening for a quick drink, but they stayed till the end of the show, and now she was congratulating me for winning the big cup, I told her that was no need to take the meeky, she laughed and apologized, she asked me if we could meet that afternoon down in Newquay, where we could have a coffee and a little chat, I said okay and I made it clear that in the evening I would have to be on duty, she promised that it would be only for an hour. We met that afternoon, it was nice to see her again cheerful as ever, the first thing she asked me it was about Vittoria, she thought she was with me at the hotel, I told her that we had split up long time ago. She said that she was missing me terribly and she would be prepared to find a job near me as long as we'd be together again, adding that her life in London wasn't the same without me. Unfortunately I had to tell her that I was now engaged to a London girl called Edie (even though I was not) she asked me if this girl was prettier, I said she was, and much younger too, Elizabeth didn't appreciate my answer and so she started crying, mind you I didn't see any tears, I knew she liked me but as I always thought only for convenience she always wanted me as a friend, I always had a feeling that she had someone else. She was very attractive and very clever I might say, but in all I was still thinking that I was still blaming her for losing Vittoria. We said a rather cold goodbye... she walked off without even looking at me. Never seen or heard from her again since.

The summer went by too fast, at the end of the season we went to Italy on holiday again for nearly a month, of course it was a cheap holiday as we stayed with my family, pity we didn't have a car, but then again we didn't miss it, we toured around in coaches, we visited some of he most beautiful places in Italy. Edie loved Venice, I reckon we've been there a dozen times. We sample the good food of the small little restaurants, always go in the back streets, where the workers go, sadly one month went quickly too, by the time we knew.. there we were back in the London east end.

Again I found a job in Epping in an old pub restaurant, the story goes that few years back it was frequented by Cray twin brothers, some notorious gangs I believe, I felt if I was working in Chicago, thank god March arrived so we could go back to Cornwall again.

March 1965... The season started with a bang, news came that Franco tighten the knot with Maureen, would you believe it, I thought then the fellow's gone cracker getting married to a foreigner, maybe I was jealous, and I thought sooner or later I had to propose to Edie too, but I thought I better wait. The season went quicker than I thought, I enjoyed again as I almost had the same team workers as the year before, including my second in charge David. Went back to London and I found a good job in Chelsea again in a posh restaurant as the winter before, where I could meet a lot of personalities and used my press identity card, this time I carried with me a small camera, which I used a few times, it was a real good fun, this restaurant put me up with a nice bedroom too, it was in a basement but it was very comfortable. Edie found a job in a local supermarket, and in spite of that we saw each other a lot. One afternoon I was looking into a jeweller shop as I thought to by her an engagement ring, so I did and I propose her in my digs with a small bottle of champagne, she ask me where I bought the ring, as she wanted to buy me one too, so she did, and there and then we were engaged. We started planning for the wedding, but first we had to face the 1966 summer season to put some money on the side for the big event, her mum couldn't really afford and neither my parents, but as we were going to get married in England, and as we knew the date already, would you believe it? April the first 1967. and planned to do our honeymoon in Italy, as We did not to go back to Cornwall until the 21st of April. My parents suggested at their expense that we should do a second wedding in Italy or maybe a celebration type like, so we could invite some relatives, we were over the moon about, and a date was set for that too.

March 1966   We went down to Bedruthan to get ready for the new season again, I was getting a bit edgy to do the same thing every year, I wanted to do something new, but what? I used say to Edie, I'm getting a little fed up with this, she use to say; is not all that bad, you have a good job and so do I, I thought she is right, first we must get married, and then we'll see what the good fortune will bring us. We got a phone call from Franco asking us when we were getting married, of course we could not go to their wedding as last year season was already in full swing, I was saying to Edie that we should have done a double wedding as we met you two at the same time. I suppose Franco and Maureen couldn't wait for another year. Yes, she said that would have been a good idea, but they were working in London and were working in Cornwall. Their wedding was happily concluded with a honeymoon in Italy, on their return they found a nice flat in the east end of London and Franco opened a delicatessen near Buckingham Palace, good luck to him, I'm sure he will make a fortune, mind you he's always been very tight with his money, and of course he only had his mother in Italy, that is as much as know about his lot, I know he lost his father when he was young, in saying that, he grow up quite sensible, that's why he saved his money more than I did. However, we wrote a nice card with our best wishes with a hope to see them very soon.

They reply that they looking forward to see us too, saying that they kept a bottle of spumante on the side to celebrate their first year of marriage. I thought: Big deal! I don't even like the stuff, too sweet for me, I rather have a bottle of champagne! Well...We are still awaiting for that bottle of Asti Spumante..........Some friends!!

What a season that was, I think all taken in consideration 1967 was one the best season, and my earning were better too. That year we managed to set up again the staff football team, the past years we used to play the guest, but this year we started playing the other hotels, we used to have our football pitch, which was a deserted airport not very far from the Hotel.

(On the left standing; 1. Klaus (German), 2. Michael (Swiss) 3. David (English) 4. Eugene (Irish) 5. Mario (Italian) 6. Francesco (Italian) 7. Marco (Italian)

(Kneeling from left. 8. Giuliano (Italian) 9. Gerry (English) 10. Jose' (Canary Islands) 11. Vittorio (Italian) 12. Leo (Italian) Last with dark glasses it's me 9. (Manager & Trainer)

What a Great football team that was. Klaus was one *of the chefs providing the tricks of the trade*, he was a bit of a bully boy, I wouldn't have liked to tackled him, and Vittorio the head barman, bless him he was supplying my drink every day, I loved my pint of bitter with my lunch, lives now in Italy in his mansion, he loves his garden he likes to cut the grass every week, we often visit him, and he spoils us tremendously, cooking is not is not is favourite hobby so he let me doing it, and I love it. Mario he's married to an English girl he tells me that he misses England, but I told him that he's got his Linda to keep him warm, retired and lives in Italy, he's one of the famous Pallio organisers in Siena, he's a connoisseur of good wines and he's an excellent chef, I am a bit jealous as I can't compete with him. Marco a car addict, he loved is old VW, lives in Australian now, Giuliano the chef settled in Cornwall, Eugene a great Irish friend of mine sadly passed away in Germany a few years ago, the rest I lost touch, except I remember well Jerry the drummer, he was the best for me as he was my driving instructor too, so when we went back to London I had my driving licence in my pocket, but I didn't have the car.

One day out of the blue, my boss, Peter Whittington came into the restaurant one morning, actually every morning he used to spend a few hours in the kitchen too as it was his favourite hobby, anyway, he was holding these bunch of keys and told me to move my car, I looked at him as if I was dreaming and so he repeated himself: "Would you mind to move your car please?" It's was just outside the kitchen! I took the keys and I went out and saw this new Viva Vauxhall, I nearly fainted, yes my boss bought me a car but I insisted that I should pay him back, he told me that wasn't very important, but he said that I deserved it. I did pay him pay it back though, with my retainer, because I 've always been proud of myself to be independent. At the end of the season we went back to London again, but this time with our own car, no messing about with train, I told Edie that I was glad of going by car just in case I would meet another girl on the train, one is enough... she told me that if I would say another word she would divorce me before we would get married. Her mum was very proud of us, so I had no problem to live in their house rent free. Actually it was quite a big help, so we could save a little bit more for that special occasion.

Chapter 16
A beautiful Italian style wedding

1967 So much for our wedding planning, maybe we were looking forward too much for that special day, but sadly In January I received a telegram that my father had died, few days later I was back with my distraught mother, she was incredibly broken in pieces, they have been together for over fifty years, and never once they went anywhere without being on their own but always together. Edie couldn't come with me but her and the family were thinking of us, I stayed a few days with my mother and promised that Edie and I we would join her after the wedding which would be on the first of April 1967. she was so happy to hear that but she said that the second ceremony would not take place without my father. I told her that wasn't important, one ceremony was good enough for my marriage.

(My beautiful wife and I on our wedding day 1st April 1967)

It was a very sunny day, the wedding was as expected but none of my family came but I was happy that my good friend Dany came from Italy especially to be my best man. We had a lot of guests including my friend Mike and family and of course another Italian living in London my good friend Armando from Lake Garda, who at the time he had his first restaurant in London to run, but took the time off too be present at our wedding We had the reception in an Italian restaurant in Leytonstone, and that made it a very Italian wedding, of course we spent the night in a hotel in Epping, it was a nice hotel as we had the television in the bedroom, a very rear thing in that time and funny enough we just couldn't go to sleep so we watched a film, and who ever read this please don't laugh, the film was called; "The diary of a chambermaid" I said; "Our bloody job seems to follow us everywhere we go!" We laugh and we were happy that we had a wonderful day, but sad to think that my father would not be there to our next visit. The next day we caught a train from Vittoria, we planned to stop in Paris for two nights, Dany was with us of course, as he had to be back to Italy to his own restaurant. We had a lovely day in Paris which was very nice, and had some fabulous meals and see lovely places, Dany is a great company, and we were very glad to have him with us. We caught the train to Brescia and a day later we arrived home, and happy to see my mum, which we found her rather frail, still very sad for the loss of her greatest love. My sister who was living in a flat down below, said every time she was going upstairs to see mum, she would find her in tears.   Of course the second celebration was cancelled, we didn't mind at all, we were as much happy to be with mother and keep her good company as anything else. We took her around to see many places which she never seen before but it wouldn't make any differences, she just wasn't interested, I will always remember that one day she told me; not to be surprised, if before the year ends she would join my father, true to this day, she died two weeks before the year ended To end our staying a lot of my relatives invited us for dinner or lunch, and I must say we had a wonderful time, although it wasn't a proper honeymoon.

January 1968... Another telegram, saying my mother had died, I had to go down very quickly, as usual I was there after two days the funeral already took place. I stayed a week to get the flat straighten up because it was my intention to rent it to some summer tourist, so I could get some money for the house as I had to sell some land which I acquired when I was working In Switzerland. After I got the flat in good order I gave the keys to my sister, and told her what I wanted to do, she was more than please to look after it. As soon as we arrived back ion England we packed our car up and we went to Bedruthan, the hotel was already in full swing, my assistant David had done a good job to keeping the staff under control. Everyone was pleased to see us, and I must say they played a few funny jokes in the new bedroom we were allocated. Although we were happy sleeping in our new quarters, it wasn't the same than living in a proper house. One day we went to visit a little village very near to the hotel called St Mawgan, it was absolutely a dream village we just loved it, parked our car and looked around, we noticed that they were building new houses, right in the centre, they were lovely three bedrooms ones with the garage, and the price was very reasonable I thought, only £2, 900 it's a laugh really, now days the same house is nearly £300.000, we went back to the hotel, and I was talking to my boss, and he said to me that he had an idea of how I could buy that house, he asked me all the details, I had the brochure which I picked up he just said leave that to me , few hours later he gave me a letter, and told me to go up the council to see the house department, and so we went and we met this councillor, gave him the letter, and two weeks later we had the mortgage to buy the house, few months later we moved in, cleaning the wooden floors and varnishing them   as we could not afford the carpets, and to our beds we had two orange boxes as beds side tables, later when the hotel threw out some old carpets I would put them in the car, and use them up stairs in the bedrooms, believe me they were good enough to serve the purpose, (Now days' newlywed   they wouldn't dream to adapt themselves to such humility)   but somehow we managed and very soon we had a lovely house even to envy many people now days, which we liked it so much.

That summer we advertised my Italian flat, and we managed to get some customers, only for two months of the present summer, that was a start and I suppose, I told my sister to keep a note of the expenses that the following year we would come down and put everything strait, as bought the a new house we couldn't afford to go on holiday again, instead Edie's mother came down to see us for the 1968 Christmas holidays and soon we were at the beginning of 1969 season trying our best to put together a few pennies. And during the summer of 1969 we tried to advertised the flat again this time we managed to rent for four months, which gave us some extra income, and the last guests we had were leaving the middle of September.

1969 the end of the season was approaching and we thought of starting a family, as planned Edie was pregnant, but in October we went to Italy for the first time by car, I must have been crazy to travel on them roads, with Edie in them conditions, of course there were no motorways then in France and very few in Italy, It took us two and half days to reach our destination, what a struggle, but we made it and it was truly one of the best holidays we ever had then. when we arrived we put our accounts right with my sister and my brother in law.

My brother and my sister and their families were pleased to see us, likewise we were over the moon, and they were thrilled to hear that there was an addition to the Laffranchis families. Going down by car it was quite an experience, considering my little driving knowledge, it was very exciting, visiting friends and relatives, but two weeks were not enough, still we travelled back to England with lots of goodies which then you couldn't find in our shops, or if there were any they were too expensive, like parmesan, olive oil, liqueurs and a few bottles of wine, of course being in the catering business I did like to live the continental way, like Bedruthan Steps food was undoubtedly one of the best in England, although not recognized by the catering industry, but this Hotel was always full with regulars coming back year after year and I can vouch for that and the creator was Peter Whittington whom put on the English map the glorious Continental way of living, a real food expert.

(The telly chefs' celebrities)

He was infatuated, perhaps in love with the French cuisine, his king chef was none the less Robert Carrier, who I still think he was the best unlike a lot of rubbish that you see on telly now days, dirty, with long hairs, unshaven, with beards, never wear a proper hat, a white jacket, or an apron and finally swearing all the times.... no need for that at all...... For goodness sake men, just do your bloody cooking and shut up!! We are talking about food here!! What's wrong with you people?

Chapter 17
Welcome to our first son

1970. As usual the season at Bedruthan Steps was again in full swing, regarding the staff, we had almost the same lot, mostly Italians and Irish, not many English, in fact English males waiters were very rear in the sixties, they don't like to be servants, that's what my brother in law told me once when he was looking for a job and I offered him to join me, in saying that the females are different, I found that they adapted themselves to catering business more than the boys, come to think of it, we had some lovely girls working at Bedruthan... and very reliable too.... I will say no more.

It was a Wednesday, that day we had a dinner and dance, that was the money maker day for the Whittington's, every dinner and dance we had to transformed the restaurant completely, it was quite a hard afternoon to set it up, the restaurant became like a musical stage, it was really fantastic. Towards the end, I guess that eleven pm my good friend Prufer that was the general manager, received a phone call from the Truro Hospital to say that my wife had a boy, even before giving me the news Prufer wrote a big notice and stuck it on the restaurant door that said in big letters "IT'S A BOY" then of course he passed on the message, and I left everyone else to their job and I went to see our new baby boy. You might say that he has grown fast, I am cheating really. I found the baby and Mum were in good health and of course we were over the moon.

I stayed a few hours and then I was asked by the head nurse to leave as the young mum needsed a rest, so there I was back at the hotel in no time at all, where I foud a crowd of my good friends, organising a booze up. I felt a bit heavy in my head in the morning as I don't usually get very tipsy, but it was a good celebration.

(Little Paul, Mum and myself)

Mum Edie and the baby came home a few days later, of course a little much smaller than on the previous page, naturally life started to be a little different, Edie was very busy with the first baby so I had to see to some of the other chores, I had no problem with the washing up, as that was my first profession since I was born, somehow I had a problem doing the other washing or changing nappies but in the end everything seemed to be alright. My job at the hotel kept me very busy, in fact we had one the busiest summer of all times, the end of the season came soon enough, not for us though as we really couldn't afford a holiday that year, the baby was too young to travel, then of course my boss decided to keep open the Three Seasons Restaurant, which was below the Hotel, during the summer this one was used only for outsiders and guests who wanted a special meal for special occasions. For the winter it was decided to run the three Seasons during the winter months at a special offer, which it meant two persons having dinner would qualify for a free bed and breakfast for the night, of course it was a bargain, mind you it was only operating three days a week, full weekend, the rest of the week I was working in the office or doing other jobs, so, practically I was working seven days a week. I was on my own serving and clearing up, and get up early in the morning to do breakfasts for the qualifying guests. All this for less wages than I was getting during the summer, Yes I was getting £25 a week, and that wasn't enough to pay for my mortgage and other things and we had a baby as well to feed. considering that Edie wasn't working I wasn't very happy really and I found it very hard. One day I saw an advert in a catering magazine for a position as a Restaurant Manager in a Hotel in Kent, I said to Edie, bloody hell it is a bit far away if I get the job, she said that there was no other way, if I ever get the job we would have to sell the house. I applied and I went for the interview, it was the White Cliffs Hotel in Dover, I came up from Cornwall and I had to stay with my mother in law for the night, and travel down to Dover in the morning, I was the last to arrive for the interview and there were eight applicants, I was the last to be interviewed, I honestly thought I had no chance to get that job, but I was wrong, I got the job with double the wages I was getting and with living accommodation until we would find a house in Dover. Of course my knowledge of French language did help me, as the general Manager was Belgian, and he interviewed me in French, I was given a month to start my new job, that suited me fine. On my journey back I rung Edie from a phone box, and she was over the moon. The next day I went to see Mr Whittington and I gave him my notice. Such news wasn't very welcomed, especially the 1971 season was very imminent, and of course it wasn't easy to find a new Restaurant Manager, but I was very honest to tell him the offer was too good to be refused, further more it was an all year around job with full wages, unlike Bedruthan in the winter my wages would be cut down in half.

Peter Whittington was very upset to lose me, funny enough he never had boys in his two marriages, only girls, sometimes he treated me like almost a son, once he even said to me that I had shares in his company, but I've never did seen any, I couldn't even get a proper rise when I asked him, and that was quite a few times. In saying that, he did treated me well over the years, but whatever he gave me I paid him back with my hard work. Talks went on for a few weeks until my boss offered me the same money all year around as I would get with my new job, as I was committed to the new job he offered Whittington an alternative, meaning to have aperiod trial for a couple of weeks, if I didn't like the new job I would come back to Bedruthan, and of course I wouldn't put the house on the market yet. He agreed and we shook hands.

Three weeks later Prufer rung me up and asked if I had made a decision yet, I said yes and said that I was staying in Dover, I told him to tell Peter that I apologized for the inconvenience, if he had anything to say to me he could have really rung me himself, instead of having you as post master, Prufer told me that I was completely right on that point after all, I told him that I gave over eight years of my life to Bedruthan. Prufer said:"I wish you good luck Julian, I think I would have done the same."We put the Cornwall house up for sale, Edie and Baby Paul were living in London with mother May and I started to work in Dover At the White Cliffs Hotel a very well know hotel all over the world, I was given a first class bedroom on the first floor of the hotel as a temporary accommodation until I would find a house, the staff really made me feel very welcomed, well, there were a few at first that didn't like me that much, but I suppose you get this when you take over a top management job. Yes, I could see that I had a good job and I was treated as a real Restaurant manager, I had my office and my own secretary Lesley, she was really marvellous and beautiful for that matter I liked her very much, she was very helpful and thoughtful in every aspect, she'd do anything for me, even extra working hours, with tea or coffee always at hand. I had a day and half off a week so I could travel up to London to see Edie and Paul. My mate Eugene was working in London then, for a classic international food guide Ronay as he was off on a Sunday he would pick up Edie and the boy and popped down for lunch at the White Cliffs, it was wonderful to be able to sit down and have my lunch with my family, and be served like royalty. I certainly wouldn't have been able to do that at Bedruthan Steps Hotel.

Chapter 18
Goodbye to St Mawgan's house

June 1971. Six months went by, our house in Cornwall was sold so we had to store our furniture because we just couldn't find any property in Dover that would suits our needs, in fact there were none at all. One day I noticed just outside Dover they were building these houses and people were queuing up night and day to reserve one, I had no time to queue up, fortunately the agent who was in charge of the sales, used to come for lunch where I was working, I asked him, and he told me that for the moment phase one was all sold, I was not in a hurry, as a matter of fact the General manager transferred me to a beautiful flat on the ground floor to the hotel Annex overlooking the sea and he told me to feel free that I could have had the wife and the baby joining me, but Edie would rather wait and stay with mother. I did miss them both, but in all it wasn't that bad, it gave me a change to get used to the new environment. I had quite a responsibility and a very large team of waiters and waitresses and also out catering functions to organize. It wasn't an easy job the outside catering, but once you knew how to do it was easy enough.

I was taking some lunch time orders, when my special; customer came in could see he had a smile on his face, he just whispered "It's your lucky day Julian a chap just changed his mind on a new property in Newlands, if you want it come to my office this afternoon with your cheque book, I need a small deposit to secure the property. He didn't have to tell me twice, that same afternoon I went to

see him and put my deposit down, without even look at the house. The next day I went to see the property, it was on the first cull de sac. A lovely three bedrooms house with the garage and garden, to be completed in a couple of months. I just couldn't wait to ring Edie. Luckily she rung me that evening. She was over the moon, I was a little fed to live like a bachelor. While I was waiting to move in, I used to go in the hotel workshop to prepare some work that I was going to put in the house, like skirting boards, I wanted a special ones, shelves, and other few little things, and I did enjoy doing these jobs as they kept my free afternoons busy, nearly every day I used to go there and take some measurements, obviously with the Forman permission.

We moved in Newlands just before my first year at the White Cliffs Hotel, we loved it, the first day we move in I laid on a surprise for Edie, a new colour television, it was a novelty then not many families had that, I made sure that they deliver it the same day we moved in, and our furniture arrived from Cornwall before eleven in the morning, I always remember that the day before I went up to London to pick up Paul and Edie and while we were driving down we noticed the van with the name which had our belongings, of course we got there before, as I already had the keys with me, we enjoyed getting everything ready, from the garden and the rest, actually they gave me a few days off to get us straighten up, so everything turned out fine.

I was only at the White Cliffs for over a year when one morning the general manager called me in his office and he said that a new Government law just came out, like anyone being in management had to have a certificate from the Government Catering scheme department, and without this certificate I would not be able to be a Restaurant Manager any longer in England, unless I went to a course at a college in Canterbury to pass a tutorial exams to get such Diploma, I had no problems, the hotel would pay my wages, which they would get that money back anyway, so off I went to the college the following Monday. As I got there I saw that

I wasn't the only one, there was about a dozen of us, I presumed from others hotels around Kent. The teacher was a nice chap, he was showing us how to organize parties and some other chores. He got to the restaurant service when he showed us how to slice an orange with knife and fork and making it a star on the plate, he done that alright and then he asked if any of us knew how to do it, I put my hand up, and okay, I did it faster than he did, when the lesson finished he asked me to follow him to the director's office, I thought, something's going on here. The Director told me that I didn't have to come back as I did pass my test, and they will send me the certificate and they will let the hotel know that I passed. I said thank you very much, I really appreciate that....Goodbye and off I went, taking the rest of the two weeks off getting more jobs done in our new house.   I made a lot of friends working at the Hotel, from customers to workers, a particular one was Francisco, he was Spanish and he was the head barman, and I must say that he was very helpful to me when I took over as a Restaurant Manager, he used to introduced me to the regular customers and some of the unpleasant staff started to like me as I was quite lenient to them, I was never nasty, sometimes I hated to see the Chairman acting as if he was Hitler. Once I had a very attractive young girls serving drinks in the bar, she was wearing a mini skirt and she was offering a nice smile to all the customers, males or females, I suppose that was her job as people used to enjoy looking at her, not so much Mr Johnson the Chairman as he caught my eye and call me over and very nastily he ask me to sack the girl as she was dressing disgracefully. I told him that I couldn't do that, he said I could because that was an order from the boss, I replied gently to him that we should not argue in front of he customers, if he didn't mind to go to his office, then we could sort out the matter so much at ease. He entered the office first and sat behind his desk, he really loved that desk, I suppose he felt his high authoritarian behind that. He asked me to sit, I told I would rather stand as it would not take that long to sort out that problem. I told him strait; "Who do you really think you are?" He looked flabbergasted, and then calmly said that the girl did not look right in that skirt. I told him that he jus couldn't go around a sack employees just like that, I pointed out that we are in the 1970s and not in the 1870s, plus I said we had law that we were not able to sack anyone unless we wrote two warning letters, naturally, if an employee would do something really nasty then we could dismiss him or her on the spot. He was quite surprised that I knew that particular law, and of course he knew it as well, so there and then he fully agreed, and told me to sort it out the best way I could, he asked me to have dinner with him that evening, we had two lovely Dover soles with a bottle of vintage Chablis.

After dinner I summoned the girl with the mini skirt and told her that she should wear a little longer one, she apologized and from then on she dressed properly. Shame really, I bet everyone missed seeing them two lovely legs walking around...no doubt including myself.

One evening I was walking around the restaurant to ask everyone if everything was to their satisfaction, I noticed there was this lady, maybe in her sixty's or more, she was beautiful and smartly dressed, I asked her if everything was alright, and she kindly smiled and asked me: "I bet you don't remember me!" I was quite surprised and I said no, probably without thinking, and she said if the name Sonya reminded me of someone I knew, I kept looking at her and then all of a sudden I remember The May Fair Hotel that's where I met her... Yes she was Harry Roy's wife, and I remembered that she served us drinks in her bar's house in Montague Place. Later we sat in the lounge and we talked about our little past and lived to meet her famous husband and herself. I knew that Harry had left the May Fair Hotel to open his own place the Empress Club in Bond Street and

Mike Mackenzie was playing the piano there, I used to go and see him, of course I was not a member, but I had the permission of Harry that I could go in as many times as I wished. Sonya was not there very often, maybe a few times a week. She told me that she left Montague Place long ago, as the place was too big for her, she went to live in a very secluded Mews near the May Fair and now she spends her time visiting places around England. She finally add that a lot of her friends disappear very fast. She was leaving the next day, she gave me her phone number and asked me to pay her a visit when in London. But I really never called her, sometimes I wished I did, I suppose I was too busy to enjoy my family and our new house.

Thank god I had a car that gave me the chance to run where ever I wanted to, sometimes in spear time I used to go fishing with some friends of mine, but all we could catch it was macackerel, a terrible hard fish, hard to cook, and tasteless, but we used to enjoy it in Francisco's house.

Raffaele who followed me from Cornwall, he was a real friend, he's another one that was planning to get married, but it had go to Italy, time arrived for him quite early to tighten the knot, so off he went and a month later he came back with a wife, she worked in the hotel with him as a chambermaid, but I don't think she liked that very much. I'm still in touch with Raffaele and his wife, I understand they have now a very nice restaurant near Naples in Italy. We ring each now and then and he keeps asking me to pay him a visit.... Yes, I would like too, maybe one day I will.

Chapter 19
A short visit to Cornwall

July 1973 Franco and I and the wives decided to pay a visit to Cornwall by car, we went to visit the Whittingtons in their Mansion, their reception was quite cold and after a cup of coffee we left rather disappointed, Franco had improved his financial statues with his delicatessen by then, and I was still a Restaurant Manager, never the less, the Whittingtons wouldn't have hurt themselves to compliment me, instead Whittington said to Franco that he would have liked to open a business in London, Franco told him that he was not interested as he was quite happy with his present business. I suppose Whittington did that to make me jealous or perhaps being spiteful, I know he was still hurt by me leaving the firm. He never heard or spoke to me since. I was some kind of sorry for such dreadful parting. A few years later Whittington and Mary were in London enjoying a few weeks breaks, they used to enjoy their visits to the many theatres' shows, of course at that time they had bought a place in a mews, so they used to stay there quite a few times, on day he had a terrible stroke that damaged his brains and he was in a wheel chair for almost twenty years, I was told this by a friend of mine who was in touch with them. I rung a few times to one of his step son nice fellow Nicholas, and of course he kept me informed.

I was quite happy in my job, for the moment I had no choice, but of course in life you want to improve yourself, we had some money on the side, which we saved from the sale of our house in Cornwall, we were always thinking to do something with, like opening a little restaurant or maybe something smaller, we kept looking around. Edie suggested that I should stick to the White cliffs as it was giving me a good wages, so we didn't have the problem of running a business and probably go bust, I thought about a delicatessen, as the continental specialities were taking over the food market, this is why Franco made a mint for himself, but of course he had the right position, London and near Buckingham palace, he couldn't go wrong there, but he was afraid of the IRA problems at that time as they were bombing London quite often, he even thought to start a business out of London, that way he would have been far from those atrocities. Instead he changed his mind, he sold the shop and started a business in South kensington, he a very large coffee bar, which apparently it was another mint for him, he had quite a few staff, and I don't really know exactly what happened there, but he divorced Maureen and remarried again with a Colombian girl, whom she gave him a pair of twins, I'll say no more.

September 1973 still working at the White Cliffs, and I must say I still enjoy it every minute of it, I had a lovely job, a lovely family, lots of friends where we were living, we used to have a very happy and good social life, as years started to go by, Edie and I thought, if we want to have another child we should not wait any longer, so we decided for another one, and that was a real perfect timing because on the 27 of May 1974 our beautiful boy Peter came along,

(Our son Peter with his favourite friend)

he was a chubby little fellow, there we had two boys born on the same day of the same month with four years apart, that was a remarkable coincidence, and yet, the date was only a week away from my birthday, I wonder if it's hereditary or just coincidental, as my sister and my cousin Marie were born on the same day, same year too, in this case my mum and Marie's mum were sisters. I did say that was a perfect timing. Peter and Paul started to grow and well behave boys.

We couldn't go on holidays abroad for two or three years as the boys were too young, but we used spend some time in London with Nan May, and they used to enjoy that, naturally she used to come down and stay with us many times, so Edie and I could spend some time shopping around without having the two troubles around us, but we used to miss them every minute. came by and disappear very quickly, sometime you thought nothing of the time, but when passes you by you realize that you haven't achieved what you really wanted to do, never the less, we were happy and I still had a good job at the White Cliffs Hotel and that was more than important.

September 1974 we had a surprise visit from my sister and her family, it was a surprise alright, you can imagine we had three bedrooms, and there were five of them, I said to Edie this is going to be an impossible situation, however, we had some sun beds an bunk beds, in the end we solved the situation. It was nice to see them, and we tried our best to give them the very best, we took them around a bit, but as they had their own car they visited a lot of places themselves in Kent, and they enjoyed themselves quite a lot. We had some beautiful dinner in our house and with the arrival of Peter they were over the moon. We introduced them to a lot of our friends, but of course there was the problem of the language, but luckily their son

Mauro spoke a bit of English, and that was very helpful when they went out on their own. They stayed for a couple of weeks, I thought they were the longest weeks of our lives, but never the less we put up with them the best we could. On the day of their departure we went down to the port to say bye, bye, they were so pleased.

We gave a few packs of English tea, as at that time in Italy it was quite expensive, also I gave my brother in law a couple of bottles of gin as I introduced him to the gin and tonic, he never had that before in his life and he loved it. We promised that we would see them the following year, what a fantastic family. As I am writing this, my sister is still alive, she'll be ninety this year, sadly we cannot go and see her because of this Corona Virus that is destroying the world. Let us hope that everything will be back to normal soon.

Chapter 20
A very lucky opportunity

In the spring of **1975** I was offered by some local restaurant owners, if I was interested to become their partner in opening an Italian Restaurant in Dover, at the time the town didn't have any restaurants of that kind, they were told about my knowledge and experience, and of course they needed someone like me, (I'm sorry to a big head) without thinking twice I accepted, I cannot disclose my capital of money, but I can tell you that my shares were 33% and a bit, but shares of profits 50% as my job was responsible the complete running operation of the joint. Once again came the big problem, of course to give my notice to the White Cliffs Hotel, and it became a nightmare, as the management, three directors and a Chairman, as the Hotel was run as a trusty, for an old family residing then in France called the Lyons, nothing to do with the old Lyon of the 1950 cafeterias chain. Anyway my notice was accepted but with a little bit of bitterness, the Chairman offered me more money to stay, but I said that I was moving to Italy for good, that made it more simpler and being accepted it. The new restaurant was going to be just across the road from where I was working, and of course the name was already fixed over the front, but a week before the opening date, I thought the front near the door needed a bit of more paint, and as I was doing that (I didn't have to but I tried to save a few bobs) my ex White Cliffs Chairman was crossing the road, and saw me, but never said a single word. I was told that he was furious and I will not write the names he called me, as he knew that the new restaurant was probably damaging his business, because he knew that over the years I acquired quite a good will at the old White Cliffs.

We called it "The Ristorante al Porto" the day of the opening was to be on the 27 of May the birth of my two boys, couldn't have been a better coincidence but it's true I thought to do only a wine and buffet reception with ofcourse some Italian specialities like; lasagne, cannelloni, parma ham and someother delicacies. I invited 120 people from businesses to non business people which I met and served at the White Cliffs Hotel, and also many from Freight companies down at the port and of course some news reporters covering most of Kent area. the opening was very successful, and from the next day we started operating seven days a week, we needed the money, and of course that started to come in quite nicely. The first few weeks I started to have problems with the chef, which the one we had he wasn't at all that good and he was very temperamental, so I had to borrow the one who was at the White Cliffs, it was a lady and she had retired a few months before I left, anyway she was kind enough to help us out, but one day as I was walking in town I met an Italian friend of mine called Tony, who used to work at the White Cliffs as a chef long time ago, he was telling me that he was now working in this small fish restaurant and wasn't very happy, so I offered him the job there and then, a week later he was my chef for my great

(Ristorante al Porto)

Restaurant. Tony was a stranger to my menu, so with a bit of training he soon picked up everything, he became soon accustomed to the place managing easily to cook almost all the recipes my way, people would only come in to eat his cannelloni and his lasagne without mentioning the fresh tagliatelle which they were one of our top specialties. Tony was with me more than twenty years and over the years his two sons also joined our team. Next door to us there was a butcher which supplied our finest meants, we like it so much that a year later we bought the premised, really, lovely old butcher decided that he wasn't getting too many customers where he was, he thought to take his business up town, indeed he was right and we were right to buy his premises, making the restaurant bigger, and better with a new cocktail bar and a little lounge where we could sit people waiting for a table, also we added a new party room, as we needed it for the Christmas time parties and weddings.

Summer 1976. We were busier than ever, sometime during the summer months we had a queue outside, and also we were booked solid a couple of weeks in advance, almost all year around. We were not the most expensive and I'll be honest I did not wish to be in any of the food guides, but since one day I was approached by an American couple who were dining in my restaurant, they asked me if I would be interested to be in an American food guide, my first reply was: "How much would it cost me?" They said nothing, and they added that they would send me a free book as soon as it would be published. They were touring many towns in Europe to sample various food's restaurant recipes and prices, I said yes, and two months later I received a book called "Fromer Food guide" it was very nice indeed, and they gave us a very good review. I always thought the best advertising that a place can get is through the people's mouth, I don't particularly like or agree

about these Michelin starred restaurants, whether for their food or their service, and they charge astronomical prices, amongst the many I tried, I'd like to mention the last one towards the end of 2019, I ate fish with steak knife the men got served before the ladies, atmosphere nil, in all a very mediocre meal. And so were the rest I have been visiting believe me, I was very disappointed, I would suggest to some of these celebrity chefs, (I did say that before, so forgive me for repeating myself) to be more presentable and clean as you never see them wearing a hat, all you can see is long hair and unshaven faces, and please don't tell me that some hair cannot fall in some the pots and pans, or perhaps from beards, let alone big eye brows like mine. Well, in saying that, I must make a small correction to my critical view, yes I have a favourite Michelin one star Restaurant, and unfortunately is in Italy on the Lake Garda the place is is remarkable, they have had one Michelin star no more, (the owner told me that he doesn't want another one) for a number of years, Dany, that's his name , is a good friend of mine, but the chef is non the less, his wife Maria, she is no doubt the best, he can't cook for toffee, he does however do some desserts, but he is a master of his wines, which of course he has a vast good wine list, it is most important in a good restaurant..of course that's another rip off. WINE! Some restaurants tend to over price their wines, that is one question that I have been asking myself all these years, why, oh why, do they have to charge three or four or five times more than they pay for a bottle of wine? I simply cannot understand their greed!

January 1978 Next door to the butcher we had a delicatessen, one day I was talking to the owner, and I said that the place was falling apart, must admit those few properties were at least over one hundred years old, my headwaiter was living on the top flat of the restaurant with his wife and one I had to up and see him for something, they had the record player playing, and suddenly as a lorry went by along the road below, the needle of the player whizzed across the LP. I started laughing, and my headwaiter said, "we get that all the time, every time a lorry goes past during the night we wake up too!" well.... I said, "I think very soon we'll have to knock down the bloody lot!" and that gave me an idea. Few days later I had a meal with a friend of mine, whom he's a builder and a semi architect, and I mention the idea of knocking down the three old properties and build new ones, he agree with me according to the size of land

(The Restaurant's entrance

they were laying on, three massive buildings could have built on it. I suggested this to my silent partners, but they wouldn't agree, it was sad because at today's prices they would have been worth between three to four million pounds, I always had a good vision when investing, it's a pity I was born poor, but my mother gave me that precious gift.

Chapter 21

Proud of my Restaurant

March 1980. Once again I met my delicatessen neighbour, I noticed that he looked very miserable, he asked me how was the restaurant business, I said it couldn't be better, he told that he wished he could retire as he had enough of battling with his shop, in other words he didn't have many customers as he used to. He was in his sixties, I told him that he didn't have to put up with all that palaver, at his age he should sell up and enjoy some semi retirement, I think he agreed on that, then again I said you name the price we are interested to buy your place. The next day he came around with a price, and I told him that I will instruct my solicitor, I was definitely interested to buy him out. I contacted my partners, they agreed, of course the Al Porto was going to pay for it, but I didn't mind, it was a good investment. That went through in a couple of months, and after some refurbishment we open an hamburger and pizza restaurant, totally a different business than mine. My partners said to me that I had enough on my plate so they would run the new pizza place, I told them that I would expect some profits out of it as I was paying the mortgage from the profits of the Restaurant.

One morning I told Edie that we should have a bigger house, perhaps with a bigger garden, as the business was doing well, I thought I've had enough of letting the banks enjoying my fruits, I always believe to invest money in bricks and malta, that's what my father used to tell me, apart from the fact that he could never do that, but he saw what I did when I was 18 and working in Switzerland, as I was earning good money, he was the one to suggest that I should buy a piece of land, so one day I could build my own little house, (I still have the architect's drawings) unfortunately as I mentioned before that dream never materialized as I had to sell the land to pay off some alteration my father's done to the house when he retired, naturally the reason was he died so I got stuck with the bills, my brother had four children to feed and my sister had three and neither of them had two pennies to rub together, if anything they kept asking me for loans, which of course I couldn't afford all the time. After months of searching, we finally found the one we wanted, they were still building it, so we could put the deposit down and wait until it was ready. I was busy with the restaurant, but I tried to take some time off and enjoy it with the family, I had a very good staff team, and Tony my chef he was now more or less my manager, because I could take as many days as I wanted with my family that I was pretty sure that place would run as usual if any better, his two sons Michael and Lino were very hardworking boys. To be fair I made Michael more or less in charge and Lino was his assistant, sometimes they had a few quarrels, but that is normal amongst brothers, then of course they were a bit jealous of each other, but they always done their job no matter the situation.

(This was the front cover of our menu)

Yes, I was proud of my menu, I designed it, and I thought it was well presented, later printed in blue leather the choice inside was mixed or shall I say crossed with and Italian cuisine and a touch of the French one, for instance I had escargots, snails and the fabulous coquille St. Jacques.

I was told they would not sale, I just could get enough, or my Pepper steak flambé with succulent cream sauce cooked in front of the customer, and the very best was the chateaubriand with a touch of garlic and of course the sauce béarnaise who wanted it. During the winter I used to do evenings with only a couple of specialties to choose from, like the (Fillet of beef) Chateaubriand evening I used to marry it with a saltimbocca alla Romana which was Veal cooked in white wine with ham and cheese on the top, evening like that I would run out of fillet steak and Veal for sure, and I made sure that every table had an Italian liqueur with their coffee and naturally some amaretti biscuits, perhaps this was one of the reason that I was very busy, sadly you don't get nothing free now days, especially in pubs they even charge you for a slice of bread, I will not mention the price of drinks, it's a complete rip off, I vividly remember that next to my premises we had a pub, well... my gin and tonic was fifty pence cheaper than theirs, and we were serving it at the table, and at the pub you had to get it yourself at the bar.... I will say no more! My wine list, obviously had the same front cover as the menu, with a wide choice of wines almost from all European countries, in that time wines from Australia, Chile and other far away nations were very rear, unlike now days you can buy wines from almost any country in the world, and I must say some of them are better than the French and Italian. My prices were very modest if I may say so. You could have a nice bottle of Valpolicella or a French Bordeaux for as little as £4.50, now days you are lucky if you get it for less than £15 and quite honestly the wine wholesale prices they have not increased

that much since then, obviously the government takes a big slice from the importers and then there's the VAT which makes it more expensive, but in saying that, we had both of these in the 1980s too, so the catering industry are ripping off everyone's pocket. The bar was well stocked up with many aperitifs and French Brandies and I had a very wide choice of vintage ports, not many people drink port now days.

1981. We moved in our new house in September, we were quite pleased, the garden was quite in a state and it took us a few months to get everything the way we wanted, finally we managed to organise a house party, where we Invited some of our customers too, and the neighbours, of course Tony provided the food from the restaurant, and that was a big help, of course there was no shortage of wines, I always like to treat my guests properly, if we have any guests for dinner or lunch I make that the wine is on the table, and I tell the people to help themselves I know how bad it is to sit in front of your food with an empty glass, sadly this happened to me many time, with quite a few of our friends, I wouldn't say they are not nice people, but they just too bloody mean with their drinks, they leave their bottle on the next sideboard or on the floor, well... I supposed that's the only way you can make your wine go a long way. One day I was reading in a Canterbury newspaper, that there was an Italian oil painting exhibition in Rochester. Out of curiosity I went to it, as I intended to buy some paintings to hang in the restaurant walls, I must admit at the time the walls were a bit bare, I had a few rubbish prints, I didn't like that. This expiation was excellent, the paintings were superb, but not many people were buying them. The organizer a certain Giorgio, was somehow disappointed, he had with him a couple of Italian painters, which cost him an harm and a leg, as for myself I couldn't buy any as I found most of them out of my pocket funds, as I was talking to Giorgio and mentioning that I had restaurant in Dover, and I wished to make it more elegant by hanging some of hi beautiful paintings, he found that very interesting and he told me the next day he would come to see me, as he had to come through Dover to go back to Italy, actually he wanted to try a good plate of pasta as he said that a couple of the places in Rochester were utterly rubbish, I said; "Say no more, be my guest, I'd like to treat you a nice plate of our beautiful succulent tagliattelle, they are our speciality." "I shall look forward to that" He replied.

On my way back I was thinking how to get some painting on the cheap side, yes, I probably afforded half a dozen, but then again that would have set me back of a thousand pound, I thought here we again, why do I have to think about my first watch every time I have to buy something expensive, that thought never disappeared from my mind, so I was determined to get a good deal with Giorgio, no matter the costs, that is if I'll see him again.

I was at the restaurant rather early the next morning just in case he was early too. Eleven thirty am. Still no sign of Giorgio, I thought.... Ah well... I presume he forgot and as I looked at my empty walls........

Chapter 22

Restaurant becomes Art Gallery

Giorgio appeared, shaked his hand and was I pleased to see him again? Yes I was! I sat with him and enjoyed a good dish of pasta together, with a couple of glasses of wine. As a business man I was thinking to get a good discount, if I bought a few paintings, but strangely enough, before I mentioned anything he came up with a beautiful idea, he suggested to leave me as many painting as I wanted to hang on my walls, for sale or return, I said that was a lovely idea, but I also added what was there for me? I meant a commission, yes he agree on that too... well lets drink to that.... we went outside, he had a big Mercedes full

(paintings exposed on the restaurant's walls)

 of

paintings we spent the whole afternoon hanging them and making a numbered price list. From that day the Ristorante al Porto was also an Art Gallery, and the local newspapers had something to say about that too, it was a complete success.

That was the beginning of Giorno's successful business too, he didn't need to do another exhibition as in a very short time he had exhibitions of   paintings hanging in most of the restaurants in Kent, and what's more he had no overhead at all, of course, all he had to pay it was a little commission to the restaurants owners, that wasn't a lot but they made the restaurant looked better and interesting, people didn't have to read only the menu, but they also admired what was on the walls.

After that his business spread as far as London and the Midlands. He was laughing alright, (He often thank me for the idea, really it was his idea, but there again if I didn't invite him for a plate of pasta, that wouldn't have happened, and he also said that I was the one who wanted the paintings on the wall. Whichever, we both gained something. The paintings on my walls were selling like hot cakes, I even sold painting to some Americans customers, of course, they couldn't take the frame with them, so I used to give them a little discount, come to think of it, I made more profit on the frames I must have in the attic more than a couple dozens of good frames. In fact sooner than I thought, I had to ring him up to bring me some more paintings. So every six weeks he would appear and collect his loot, and change over some of the paintings that wouldn't sale, as for my commission I never took any money, I would take painting instead with almost at half of the price, so over the years I've got quite a good collection.

The business was doing well more than I expected, because we were owners of the two properties next door to the Restaurant, my partners they running the hamburger place but they were never there so they had to employ a manager which was useless. They might have gone to university in their young age, but to me whether you got it or you don't have it, their father, I suppose he was like me, with very poor schooling and he came from southern Italy, settled in Scotland, started selling ice cream and made a fortune. But the hamburger place never made a fortune, I suppose it paid for itself. However I was happy in my own restaurant, furthermore I was free to make my own decisions, they wouldn't dare to interfere, I wouldn't give them the chance, and they knew that, I was in charge of the budget and the cheques book, I was the only signatory.

One day I had a customer on his own , who more or less used to come a couple of times a week, he wasn't a great spender, he always had the same meal, a large lasagne with small beer and as we were a bit quiet that particular day, we started chatting away, I asked what kind of business he was into, he said he was an immigration officer down at the port and on his spear time he was also a record producer as well as an agent for artists in need of gigs. My mind was working like a computer, I thought immigration officer, record producer, agent for artist.... I thought this chap is taking the mickee, I asked him to tell me the truth, because I never met anyone doing so many jobs at the same time, He laughed his head off and he told me that I was right to think like that, he also pointed out that there aren't many like him, he told me that if there were more , the country's economy would be much greater. He had a point there, it's a fact that if you wait for your fortune to fall from the sky, you'll wait forever. At this point I felt again to be an alien like in the fifties, no fear of that, I will emigrate to Australia if necessary...that was all in my mind of course, as he was chatting way by telling me that he already had a catalogue of twenty records productions on his label and about thirty artist on his books, and he also asked me if I needed some artist to sing in my premises he had the right entertainers for my lovely restaurant, my thoughts about aliens suddenly stopped, and I said that my restaurant was good as it was, anyway the place was not big enough to have entertainers, plus I was the clown one who made the people laugh, I certainly made him laugh with that remark, and he told me that as a restaurateur I had a great personality, I said to a job like mine you need to be like that, otherwise I might as well go and sweep the roads, yes he thought I was funny, but I stopped him on his toes when I told him that I was also a songwriter too, he asked me straight out if I play any instrument, I said yes, my instrument is the frying pan, but jokes apart, I have something that you could be interested, I thought then about my Princess Snowdrop, which has been dormant for nearly twenty years. I explained in a few words the past of my beautiful fairy tale for children of how it started to get people interested and asked him if he would like to listen to the demo, which was had done in the sixties, and of course the London publisher who was interested so much to give us a contract but for some reasons nothing materialized. He seemed to be very interested and surprised, which I supposed he never expected. I Invited him to my house for dinner which he accepted, so he could meet my wife and at the same time discuss my play. I asked him to bring his wife too, but he told me he was divorced. We shook hands and both looked forward to our next meeting.

Chapter 23

Princess Snowdrop comes to life

Before I knew there he was ringing my house bell as we expected. I introduced him to Edie and instead of the usual box of chocolates, he opened his brief case and he took out a bottle of wine, I said what normally anyone would say: "You didn't have to, really?" He replied: "Ah well in that case!" To my astonishment he put the bottle of wine in his brief case. However, if that gesture was meant in good faith or not, I just couldn't believe it, the man was definitively MEAN! (I was writing something like this in my previous pages. What's wrong with you mean people? I reckon you think wine is liquid gold!) I had to say that as I came across quite few like that, perhaps in England they have never been used to have some wine with their meals, that's probably one of the reasons they think it is purified liquid gold. Poor old Ron, he enjoyed his meal

(Princess Snowdrop front cover of the original LP)

and we enjoyed our chat. After the meal I played the recording, which he enjoyed very much, he seemed to be very interested and he also said that he didn't usually finance his artist but in my case he would go half, maybe he saw something valuable in my work, although he said he would recruit the band and the singers. (I thought, blimey he's not all that mean then!) Plus he came with the brilliant idea, as it was a children musical and the present year being the year of the child we would give some of the profits to UNICEF, sounded okay to me! I didn't really wanted to make a million out of it, especially on the first commercial recording. Got in touch with Mike and asked him to put together some music arrangements for the band, that was done very quickly and their rehearsal begun. They used to do this in the Royal Marines rooms in Deal, and the first time I went to listen with Ron, I was really impressed to hear my music come to life, from the time before i heard it only played simply by piano, although Mike's playing was distinctively good. I must admit, Ron organized everything, from the production, the children , the band, and the recording studio. We managed to get a very knowledgeable lady producer and director who trained the children to sing the songs to perfection, by November 1979 that year the LP was on sale in various shops, and the BBC local radio gave us quite a lot of air time, likewise the local newspapers, I also appear in TV with the children and the band, They were called "Tony plus Tangent" they were really excellent, all professionals. The sale of the record went very well, in fact Ron had to reorder a few thousand more. I am not sure how many we sold but I reckon more than twenty thousand, I used to sale them in my restaurant too. Schools started to produce it on stage, even as far as North Yorkshire.

I sent a copy to the Queen Mother as she was the Patron of the Kent Children charity, she kindly acknowledged it by thanking me with a nice letter for my kindness towards UNICEF. Naturally the music was daily piped in the restaurant too. But I feel to say that marketing was not done as it should have been, this of course I partly blame Ron's fear of spending too much money.

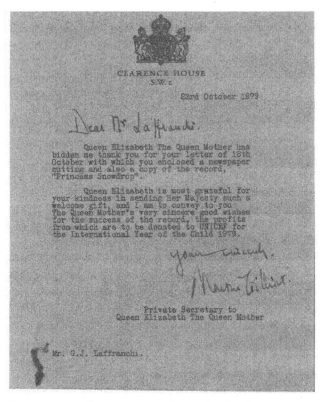

I was over the moon to have had a letter from the Queen Elizabeth Mother as I always admired her ways of doing things for her people, in fact, even my mother in law received a letter on her eighty fifth birthday, we were actually baffled for such kindness and gentle thought.

The recording was made at Foldback Studios in Deal, owned by Desmond Carrington, a well known figure, in TV and national radio, and I must give my compliments, he made my Princess Snowdrop a first class recording, Desmond was a first class professional in every sense of the word, he did not want any payment for the recording, but he expected percentage on the sale of the records which Ron promised a 10% but more studio time and money was used so Desmond demanded 20% this was not agreeable to Ron, so a big argument started. Numerous letters were exchanged between the two, which in the end it became a very sour friendship, I was in the middle of it and I couldn't do very much as I was under contract with Ron, this went on and on, Ron died a few years later, and Ron's daughter did not want to carry on with his business, and I was lucky the she reversed all my rights, and now I am the sole owner of Princess Snowdrop and other music.

At last.... We moved in "Sanrocco House" in the middle of July 1980, you might yourself ask why we called it that name, well... when it was finished we realized that we were leaving on plot 1, said to Edie; this sounds terrible, we rang our Council and asked for a number, they said they couldn't give us a number as there was far too many A and B additions to the houses number in our street, so they asked us to call it a name, which they would added to the map. Naturally there's a reason why we called it Sanrocco House and that was the only choice, as I was born in a place in Italy called that name and I was delighted to put it on the English Map.

We were rather sorry to leave Newlands, the neighbours there were very nice and down to hearth, and very friendly, we found out this to our experience, although we didn't move too far, yes, we found that our new neighbours on the left or on the right kept strictly to themselves, I wouldn't say they were unpleasant, on the contrary, it simply took them and us I suppose quite a while to have a chat, otherwise it was simply hello, good morning or good evening. At one point I thought; here we go again they don't like Aliens this lot! In Newlands quite the

opposite, when we moved in there, from both our sides our neighbours welcome us with the old bottle of milk and a nice welcome , if I may say, there was a lot of introductory hellos, small things really, but they matter so much in life, you never know when you really need a neighbours sometimes they are better than your own families. in saying that I don't know many people in our street as yet, but Edie knows them all, mind you she's a cockney and they are very

friendly people, always ready to help someone, indeed like her mother, May was a terrific woman, very gentle, she would never complain about anything, poor old girl she had a very hard life, in spite of that she had three husbands, having lost the first soon after they got married, someone else had to take over to bring the bread and butter in, times were very hard in the fifties. I remember the third husband, Percy, he was a character, he was almost blind, he could do anything he lost his sight in the second world war, they lived together for over fifteen years but then he departed too. May was 92 years old, she departed too with a smile. I can't understand why men go before the ladies, when you think of it.... It is ironic really, in life you always let the ladies go first in any situation, then to thank us, when the time comes they let us go first. Thank you ladies!

A month later we were nearly there, the garden was nicely done, and many other things, we were quite happy with the result, ready we were for a house party. Good old Tony organized the food, we had the very best and plenty wine, we invited some of our customers and of course the neighbours, thank goodness it was a sunny day, it was a fantastic day.

September 1980 I received a letter from Tonbridge a recognition by the Age of Enlightenment from Roydon Hall - The home of Transcedentalm Meditation run by the Maharishi, I believe the Beatles were involved in

such organization. Well.. couldn't be that bad, I was in line with the Beatles, with the difference that the Beatles were millionaires and I was not. However, My wife and I went as I was to be presented an award for raising money for Unicef, it was a nice presentation, at first I thought I was going to be asked to put my hand on my wallet, I was wrong nobody mentioned that, I was not impressed with their food and drinks, I don't really go for carrot juice and Brussels sprouts pie. Never the less I did appreciate their gentle gesture, I suppose you don't get an award every day.   "Princess Snowdrop" didn't make me rich and famous, it was certainly a pleasure having something published, but my thoughts were on the restaurant business, because that was definitely my bread and butter, in fact that made me aware how tricky is music business, if you don't reach the top, you die of starvation and penniless.

The restaurant was booming, and my partners came up with the idea to open a small hotel, or shall I say they found one, once again they were begging at the al Porto's door for some money, although I kept them on a diet from dishing out too much, they probably thought to get some in other ways. The bank manager was a bit upset because I very seldom borrowed money, when he used to come for lunch he used to say to his guests; "Julian is so busy that he hasn't got time to borrow my money!" Little sod does he have to tell the world about my affairs?

The place they found it was on the Canterbury road , which for over a hundred years they called it "The halfway house" I suppose the reason of that name is because the place is situated half way between Dover and Canterbury, believed to be the stop for the pilgrims on the way to the Cathedral. It has been an hotel and pub for hundred of years, and quite well known too, well situated in lovely grounds sand ample parking space.

(The old half way house how it was hundreds years ago)

Barham   The Half Way House Hotel   022 782 218

So we bought it, we refurbished it as it was neglected by the previous owner, but in the end it looked very nice, very old English style, we opened it in the spring of 1981 with a new name "The old coach house" very appropriate for its look and is position. Started off beautifully, had a good young chef, and a Spanish manager, although it was run by my partners, I used to pop in myself now and then to check that the food was done to my standards, as my partners were quite inexperienced for top class catering, forgive me for saying so but they were very good organizing sandwiches and hamburgers, they never worked in top class restaurants like I did. As I expected after six months my partners started to cut down on food quality, plus it was unfortunate that out Spanish manager left, so we had to employ another one, and business didn't seem to be the same, takings were very low, we thought that something was wrong. Very soon I found the problem, the new manager had his fingers in the till, unfortunately we found out after he had gone, I actually found the original till receipts hidden away in the barn, stupid fellow, he should have thrown them away. What a mess, fortunately a buyer came along and we sold the place, at least we got our money back, or vice versa. Never the less I found out that you cannot be in two places at the same time.

Chapter 24
A wine tour to Italy

Spring 1982 I was invited to a tour of wine tasting in Italy. What a wonderful start, we flown first class, with champagne as an aperitif, followed by a beautiful snack lunch as it was almost midday when we were flying. We landed in Forli, that's the Romagna region, this was because of the excessive sales of Trebbiano and San Giovese I achieved over the past eight months I was the number one in Kent who sold most of them. We were a a party of twenty five restaurateurs from South of England. We were welcomed like VIP people we were staying in this luxurious Hotel where in the evening we had dinner with local Mayor, (In Italy the Mayor is the most important person of each town)

(I became member of the Passatore)

t

Over here only some big cities have a town Mayor, such personality or I should say the town boss, in my town, which is Dover if I want to make a complaint I wouldn't know who to speak to, I find that wrong, if you ask me. The next day we visited the vineyards, their wines was excellent and good value for money this is why I could sell a lot, after numerous tasting we had some excellent entertaining . I was made a member of the Passatore, which is an honour, this was a very famous bandit, who robbed the rich to give to the poor, now of course are the rich to rob the poor, and they keep the money secured in their pockets. I don't expect you to laugh at my jokes, at least allow me to make a point, about Robin Hood in eighteen century, mind you did he really existed? The rest of the days we visited others vineyards, goodness me I had grapes and wine coming out of my but it was interesting to watch how they produce their wine. I must mentioned a special visit to Chianti producer Pietro Antinori, their cellars, never seen anything like it, they were really out of this world, We met Mr Antinori himself in his mansion, more like a castle I'd say in the Tuscany area, his wines are high recommendabl and quite expensive too.

On my return to Dover I had to display the restaurant the prizes I was given in recognition of my participation of improving the Italian Marketing. It was a pleasure indeed.

The following year, October 1983I was invited again, but that time to different regions. We visited the Barolo region in Piedmont and the Verona (Lake Garda) region where the Bardolino and Valpolicella is produced then we ended the tour in Rome in the Frascati region. These were the wines most In the eighties, Frascati and Verdicchio, all these were very well known in the eighties onwards. To end this I was made an honorary Sommelier, that is something that many restaurateurs don't get.

That's the regalia you get when you become a sommelier plus you get a thermometer and the silver chain with the taster. Of course I must thank my good staff for the support they have given me to achieve all this. There are many associations of sommelier all over the world, and I understand that some of them charge a lot of money to people who wants to become members, or shall I say wine connoisseurs, and of course not many can pass the test, quite a lot are being rejected. On this particular tour Edie and I took the opportunity to visit a good friend of mine on the Lake Garda, where at that time he had already established himself a member of the Michelin star recognition.

(Dany, his beautiful family and his restaurant)

Yes, we visited his beautiful restaurant "La Tortuga" on the Lake Garda, I must point out that Dany he's not one of them celebrities chefs, in fact he doesn't cook at all, he has his wife Maria that does it all. she's so special and a very good chef indeed, but she has refused many times to be acknowledged, for her inventiveness and creations, she's the real celebrity of Dany's Restaurant, of course all the family cooperates, his three daughters make sure the customers are well looked after, the eldest, Orietta is in charge, father Dany is the wine connoisseur, (He might have a Michelin star but he's not a sommelier yet) I think he's a bit jealous about that, never mind Dany I shall put a good word in for you, they might feel sorry, and promote you, in the meantime let's open another bottle of wine. Actually he did open another bottle and our meal was superb, I ought to say that instead of having grissini or bread on the table he had common crackers, which in my restaurant I served them with cheese, but there again these Michelin people want to be different than the normal ones, however, my son Peter insisted to have some bread, Maria does that too.

A truly unforgettable visit which very soon after it brought us back to our beautiful Kent, yes indeed the county of Kent it is beautiful, and so much for that reason Dover is nice too, or it was at that time, not 2020 it has become a ghost town, in the high street I counted more than 50 closed shops, i find this very sad indeed, I put so much work to keep the town on the map as beautiful as it has always been and now? Dover has so much to offer to the visitors, but sadly the local authorities are a bit blind to see this. I wonder what the cruising people think when they disembark and visit the town.

Very pleased to get back to my kingdom, I mean the restaurant so I could serve and pleased my good customers and as usual my music kept playing to my relaxed clientele while they were enjoying their good food prepared by Tony. After Princess Snowdrop more songs of mine were recorded and published by various artists. Good old Ron, he did like my music as much as he enjoyed my lasagne, he used to come in almost every lunch time, as he was working down at the Dover docks. He was very humble, he would be quite happy with his lasagne and a small beer, but many times I used to give him a glass wine too, and tell him not to be so mean with his money, he only had a daughter, lucky young Erica and his wife divorced him many years ago. I wonder why people with a lot of money don't like to spend it, are they mean? That is puzzling me. As for myself I wouldn't say I am mean with money, I am just very careful how I spent it that little I got, and of course the essentials come first.

Chapter 25
What a wondrous year

1984. My song "What a wondrous world we live in" was recorded and sung by Tony Martin, the song was played quite a lot on BBC radio 2, I was really pleased with that, I thought at last I am on the network of national radio. quite a few thousands of singles were sold and I used to play this it almost every day in my restaurant. One day there was this couple of Americans having dinner, and while I was taking their order the gentleman said to me that he heard that song before, I asked him, where did he hear that?

(The record he sent me in honour of Nancy Reagan)

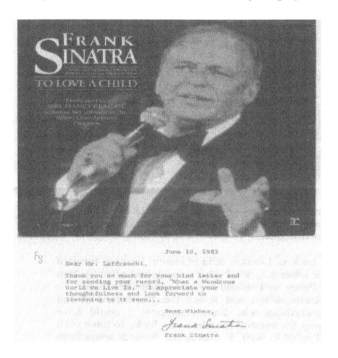

He replied that Frank Sinatra sung that song, I told that was impossible because that song is mine and that was the first recording by a male singer called Tony E. Martin and was released not long ago, he said that; he might be mistaken, but he added; that it would a good idea to send it to Sinatra, I told him that would be impossible, because Frank Sinatra wouldn't even look at it and off I went with his order to kitchen. At the of his meal I took him the bill, as he asked for, and he gave his card with on the back the private address of Frank Sinatra, and told me that he was his private electrician and added; "please send him the record and mention my name, I promise he will answer!" I wasn't very sure about that, I arrived home and told Edie about the acquaintance, she told me I had nothing to lose by sending it. So, I sent my new single to Frank and within a week he replied, thanking me for my record and he sent me one of his personal one (not for sale) that he recorded especially for Nancy Reagan, and a very special note of thanks signed by him. I just couldn't believe it, but that's how things turns out to be sometime, I think I had sent it without that chap recommendation, they might have thrown it in the rubbish bin.

1985 Life carried on as usual, the business wasn't too bad, but the summer was over. My friend Giorgio arrived with more paintings to replace the unsold ones, which it was quite nice to see my walls with a new look, but all of a sudden he started to complain about my sales, crafty sod, true I wasn't selling as many painting as the previous years, but Giorgio was getting greedy and richer, I knew he was making quite a bit of money, poor old painters they probably were struggling for a slice of bread, and he had the complete loaf for himself. I rung a few friends restaurateurs and hey told the same thing. I thought; Oh Yes? I know exactly what to do, by this time I could delegate more responsibility to my staff and then Tony was in charge anyway, so I got in the car and drove down to Italy on my own, I spent a week or so in my place, good old Irma my sister fed me, when I wasn't out with friends, she's a bloody good cook and at the same time I paid some visits to quite a few painters, there are so many on the Lake, you wouldn't believe it, and found one in the town where my friend Dany lives. I commission him to do me over fifty painting not very large but I'd say 20X12cm of all subjects, people, views etc., I was amazed that he done that within a week, the price was ridiculous, now I knew how Giorgio made his money, of course I bought some in a few shops as well, also at a good price. I took them back without the frames, as I would have never been able to put them in my car. On my last evening my sister showed me a photo she found in her attic, the picture shows my father and my brother with some other musicians rehearsing for their musical evening in 1945, probably the Germans enjoyed that too at the expense of the Italian poverty, however this is something historical which I would not part for all the

(My father, a friend, my brother, a friend)

money in the world. Arrived back in England with my new merchandise, and without losing time the next day I went to see a picture framer, (Don't really know if that is the correct name) we agreed on a price and had them all framed. Within a few days he framed me a couple of dozens, enough to cover most of the walls I was so happy with my pictures framed that I didn't wait a single day to remove Giorgio's. I put his paintings in my office, just to make sure that nothing would happen to them and put mine up, it took me all afternoon, but I was delighted to see my money on the wall, a couple of weeks later Giorgio arrived to collect his dosh, unfortunately there wasn't much to collect, as soon as he came in he noticed that his painting had disappeared, and the first thing he asked me if I had another supplier I said yes, myself, and I told him that last time he was here he shouldn't have complained, after ten years of business and I never did ask him for one penny more of commission. He agreed, and he told me that I was the best seller, even when I didn't sell a lot, finally he offered me to buy his paintings for half of list price, I wasn't very sure what to do, he said that he had so much stock in England and in Italy, of course he had an English girl friend called Penny, that's where he stored his lot, we agreed on a good price and the end he left without his paintings, With our goodbye I told Giorgio to come and see me now and then, that a plate of pasta will be always waiting for him, he said he would, but I haven't seen him since. Now I had more than I wanted, I must admit I had increased my sales as I lowered the prices, and also I told my waiters I would give them ten per cent of the list price who ever sold one, I certainly did increased the sales.

December was the busiest month for business, from the first of the month up to Christmas eve we had parties galore from business people, we had a party room with its bar and lounge on the first floor, and a party room in the next property where we had our new cocktail bar, the rest of the year we used that as a conferences room for big firms. It was very hard to do parties on the first floor, each year I would say; "That's it, this is the last time I do parties up here!" You can imagine we had to take up and down all the food and the clearing, I complained but I enjoyed every minute of it, whenever I entered my restaurant I would forget all my problems, it was like going to a party every evening, the Al Porto offered no etiquette, I wanted to see my customers feel at ease, and I didn't mind if the waiters talked to people and I kept telling them keep smiling, people go to restaurants for two things, to eat and to enjoy themselves, the majority of customers like to talk to the staff, but it's up to the staff to control themselves, not to get carried away, that is talking too much. When a customer sat down I had a waiter doing the most important job, bringing bread, gristicks butter a few olives and gherkins, so everyone would order an aperitif while waiting to order, if you don't put some food in a customer's mouth he can get very agitated. I must add that there are many restaurants now days that you get nothing unless you ask, and you'd be lucky if you get a proper napkin. Christmas went by welcoming a new year 1986... with a little snow.

We were not that busy after that very hectic December, and I can tell you I was rather pleased about it, but my chef was getting very edgy, as his main hobby was work, work, work! I told him more than once to enjoy life a bit more, I'm sorry to say that he never took his wife for a decent holiday, all he kept saying and reminding me that he had five kids to feed. In February we had an American couple coming for dinner every evening for a full week, as we were not that busy we started to chat away, and he was telling me that him and his wife were directors of a very well known chain of restaurants in America, and they were touring Europe to see places and get some ideas. (in fact he gave me his business card) he was saying that he was very impressed of the way I run my restaurant and also he liked the style of it, and he came to the point by asking me if I was interested to fly to the US, to visit his business and at the same time he made me an offer to set up in various towns restaurants like mine, I told him that was very kind of him, but I was quite happy where I was, he said that he didn't want any money from me all he wanted it was my expertise and the goodwill of the Al Porto. He said they were leaving the next day, and should I change my mind would I be so kind to write him a letter. Never thought about it anymore, but three weeks later I received a letter from his company, asking me again and all expenses paid. I replied with lots of thanks but unfortunately I could not leave my restaurant.

Chapter 26
The tenth anniversary

Spring 1986 was soon showing some flowers in our garden, but before the season begun, Edie the boys and myself set off to Spain for a short break. We had a lovely time, the boy enjoyed themselves in the swimming pool of the hotel, but time went fast, before I knew it I back at the old routine. As usual I was sharing my restaurant work with my music and Ron introduce me to a lovely singer from Thanet called Julie, she liked a few songs of mine, and I liked her voice, so Ron and I decided we would produced her first EP (that was extended play with four songs), she sold quite a few copies, and the BBC local radio gave her some air time too, but never sold as many copies as Tony Martin's single.

The tenth anniversary of the restaurant arrived with some sunshine, we celebrated in style, that day my customers had a free glass of champagne before they started their meal, they really appreciated.

(From left; Paul, Lino, me, Chris, Michael, Neil, and Tony)

plus you get a free glass of champagne. On our day off I took all my staff to the opposition, that was the other Italian Restaurant which had open a few years back, and wasn't very far from us, owned by an Italian family which I was quite friendly, and as matter of fact we always got on fine, there was no competition at all between us. We had a very enjoyable mealand I told my staff not to make any nasty comments about food or service , should there be any. As we are entitle to make mistakes, no one is perfect. Plus I gave them a little souvenir, and thank them for the good work they done.

Autumn was here again, and as usual it was time for the Beaujolais nouveau new vintage primeur, for as long as I can remember it has been famously known as some kind of race for the English wine lovers and merchants, I joined a couple of them, where we where one of the first lot to get to England with a few cases, it was certainly an achievement, there was no prize, but the first would a very nice write up in the national news, then of course it was good for my business. The Ristorante al Porto always played an important part in this, as the importers would make their first stop in Dover to sample their wine and their victory, these people were staying in various hotels, but the evening they all came to us, my place was the meeting point of the end of the race, of course I let them drink their own wine with our food without charging them corkage, but they didpay me back in the end with quite a few magnums of new Beaujolais, goodness me I had my home's cellar full of it. They'll always be unforgettable memories.

My press agent was the head reporter of the East Kent Mercury, not only I grade him the best journalist in East Kent but he was also a good friend of mine, not because he used to love my pepper steak, and our socculent scampi, but he really appreciated and admired the way and the style I run the Ristorante al Porto. He was also impressed with my music, on this particular December he said he wanted to do me a write up about the restaurant and my music, he titled a man of many talents 17/12/1987. Some times journalists tend to go over the top about someone's abilities, not Tony Arnold. My dear friend and press agent, I said to him once; "Would you mind if I call you My Press Agent?" He replied; "I would be honoured!" That is saying something.

"A man of many talents" by Tony Arnold"

"Most restaurants plays background music but the only restaurateur I know whose background music includes his own compositions is Julian Laffranchi, who owns the Ristorante al Porto in Townwall street Dover. Italian born Julian is a prolific songwriter of ballads numbers of which

have gone on record with a considerable success. Julian restaurant is well known for its distinctive regional Italian dishes. It is very much a family restaurant. Tony the head chef is excellent and has been with Julian since opening day, Tony's sons joined him as soon as they left school. Michael is the headwaiter and Lino is the wine waiter, Julian tells me with pleasure that his son Paul (17) joined him, and shall look forward to his son Peter (13) to gain some experience in the business. Julian came to this country 28 years ago. He worked in Italy, Switzerland and in many famous restaurants in London and subsequently moved to Cornwall where he met and Married English girl Edie" The article goes on endlessly. Thank you Tony!

Chapter 27
My delightful crème de la crème

1987 Yes, during those ten years or more, many things has happened, I wouldn't say everyone was good, but most of them, and so the time went by. Mainly the most fascinating were from some people I used call them crème de la crème. Here's a few stories about of them, which to me they are certainly unforgettable.

The old year had gone and spring **1988** was here. In a way I was glad to see the new year in as come February we were a bit quiet and we needed to relax and contemplate on something new, nothing much happened except in March we had a write up in The Independent one of the national top newspapers, some gastronome had picked up my Restaurant as his favourite as he found it very impressive, I was congratulated by many of my regulars. True I had quite a few whom I used to call crème de la crème, this were all residual from the old White Cliffs Hotel. They were really nice. There was this Lady, who used to come with her Rolls Royce and chauffeur George, she was very particular, when she had guests I had to provide menus without prices, as to make her guests at ease when choosing. Once she got very upset because I was not there to welcomed her, so the next day I was summoned in her Rolls and she told me off, although I told her that it was my day off, she wouldn't hear of it, she told strait that next time I should   tell her so she could change her date, no arm in that she assured me, I must add that this lady was once one the Major of London.

Mr Rogers was extremely nice he was almost like a friend, his wife was nice too and really a delightful lady, many times I invited them to my house for dinner, she used to like the way I prepared her smoked salmon, Mr Rogers used to love Cannelloni followed by my veal with parma

ham. His brother Peter the Carry On film producer use to join them in my restaurant many times with his wife Betty Box also a film producer in fifties, a very down to hearth people, quite happy to have fish and chips sometimes, pardon me, she used to like creamed potatoes, What a joy it was to served them and to know the appreciated every time they came.

Actually Peter Rogers used to like my Princess Snowdrop LP I can honestly say that he passed it on to various friends of his to see if they could use it in one of their productions. Unfortunately I was not so lucky!

How about the millionaire who used to enjoy his holidays in Dover, he was living in Dubai, and I think he had something to do with the oil business, we used to call him Champagne Charlie, actually I never knew his real name, good job he never knew too that we called that name. Of course, the reason we called him that name , it is simply when he entered my restaurant he would order me to put a bottle of champagne on every table being taken, I really thought he was joking but it turned out that he meant it. His wife would join him now and then and also his numerous family, they didn't seemed to care of how he spent his money, actually they seemed to enjoy as much as I did. on the first night of his arrival, I would never never interfered in his good and kind intentions, I tried once , just to say; " are you sure you want me to put a bottle on each table?" Hi only aswer was quite short and simple; "when money comes easy, spend it, because if you don't, who knows...."   I presume he meant; if you kicked the bucket you won't be able to spend it, good old Charlie, I've never sold so many bottles of champagne in the years the al Porto's been trading, some customer didn't drink it as they were afraid to be charge at the end, I still had to charge Charlie as I had opened the bottles as I put them on the tables, goodness me I had champagne with lunch and dinner for weeks.

It was on a summer very hot day, we were absolutely very busy indeed and when it was like that, no way I could give away a table just for one person, minimum it had to be two people, I was certain that one wouldn't get a lot of money into my till, but that particular evening a very distinguish gentleman came in and my headwaiter Michael welcomed him, but before giving him a table he came to me and said, table for one and hasn't booked, I look at this chap and said, okay Michael just give him table 8, it was a small table for two right stuck in a corner. This chap sat down, while he was looking at the menu he drunk a couple of gin and tonics, then he ordered, escargot, a dozen instead of six, and a fillet pepper steak, and a bottle of Mouton Rothschild 1970 which even then I was charging nearly fifty pound for it, now you would pay one hundred and fifty I guess, Michael said that the chap would easy spend around one hundred pounds for his dinner, I said "Jolly good, maybe we should accept singles more often!" He seemed to enjoy his meal tremendously, at the end he asked if we could do crepes suzette for one, that I said no, so he had cheese and biscuits with a double vintage port and to finish he had coffee with a double brandy. I don't know but I had a suspicion that wasn't a normal for a client to behave like that, I said to Mike, keep on eye just in case he goes out of the door without paying the bill..... well, he did asked for the bill, which I seemed to remember, that came to one hundred and twelve pounds plus ten per cent service charge which total One hundred and twenty three pound and twenty pence. He looked, and looked at the bill for well over ten minutes then he called the waiter at his table and said, that he didn't have any money and could he see the boss! Michael obliged and there I was confronting this bloody chap, and asked him what was he thinking to do, he told me; "I can't do a lot if I haven't got any money, but you can do something, you may called the police if you wish!" I told him that I would that with pleasure. He sat there with no problems, other customers didn't even realize that something odd was happening. The police arrived and one of the officer told me that wasn't the first time he was doing that, however, they told me that he will face the Magistrate in the morning. A week later I received a letter from the Magistrate saying they cautioned him and told him to pay me back one pound a month, the fellow was a solicitor, he was bankrupt and struck off the register. PS. I'm still awaiting for that money! The law is an ass!

More or less same thing happened to a friend of mine in his restaurant. (This is also a true story) The fellow who didn't have the money to pay his bill asked to see the Manager, the waiter said to him that the Manager will see you in his office. Two waiters took him to the Manager's office. After a few questions, they gave him a few hot answer and thrown him out at the back door and left him in a corner of the street rather bruised.

(One little story that might make you laugh)

One evening at about ten pm I was having my usual dinner, nothing special really, with a busy night in and out of the kitchen, tasting a bit of this and a bit of that, that Tony used to prepare and ready to be served, in a way I never felt famished for that reason many times I had to get up from my table to say goodbye to my customers and see them off with a smile. That particular evening I had this posh lady dining with some guests, Michael my headwaiter came to me and warned me that Mrs posh was leaving, obviously I had to get up to say bye, bye.... I told Michael to get her coat, he came back with it, and I said thank you grabbing her coat. Don't worry Julian I'll put her coat on, said Michael. I insisted that I wanted to put her coat on, but Michael insisted too, again I wanted to do it.... All of a sudden the posh lady (She must have been well over eighty) said: "For goodness sake boys, get on with it, when I was young everyone wanted to undress me, now that I'm bloody old everyone wants to dress me!" That was one of the greatest moments which I'll never forget.

Summer 1988. What a summer that was, we were so busy, just couldn't take any more bookings. we were fully booked every weekend for four weeks. It was a particular Saturday when to young ladies, when I say young ladies I really mean two beautiful girls, they looked very much alike, at first I thought they were twins. They came in, the time was gone past 9pm, our last order were up to ten thirty, and they asked a table for two, I said I didn't have any at all, we were fully booked, but Lino my wine waiter looked at me as to say..."Come on Julian give them a table they are so nice, they were nice with a very pleasant smile indeed, so, I offered them to eat in our little bar, we had small tables there where they were used for the people having drinks only, they said okay, and by their accent I thougth they were German or Swiss. I told Lino to get the table ready, he certainly looked very pleased indeed and he took their order too, the food didn't take long to come, toward the end I went to their table and asked them if everything was alright, they said it was superb, and told me that I should go to Switzerland and open a restaurant like

mine there, I was pleased to hear they were Swiss and I told
them that I

worked in Geneva long time ago, they didn't live very far
from there, as we chatted away they said they came to
Dover and they probably would stay for two weeks as her
brother had an accident with his motorbike and was in the
local hospital, unable to travel back. They asked me if they
could come every evening to eat, I said of course they could,

so in forth coming weeks they kept visiting us and
so we became all friendly. During their staying they
appreciated so much our friendship, that they gave the boys
a very handsome tip and of course they left me their
address. Two weeks later they sent me the above plate with
my logo painted, with a letter, thanking us for our kindness.
I found out later that one was quiet a well known painter.
we kept in contact a few Christmases. I really treasure that
plate.

Chapter 28
Two celebrations

My wife and families reminded me that I was now fifty years old and there i was joining the the geriatrics generation the have me a surprise party in our house inviting almost sixty friends, I quite honestly didn't know I

(surprise birthday party May 1998)

had so many friends, I thought it was unsual for an alien to be well liked, (Well, if any of these friend have any sense of humour they might probably understand that I'm joking) The party was great, the food was as usual supplied by Tony from my restaurant, why not, that's perks of the job, I think my invisible partner don't like that, you might ask who's this invisible partner then? Well..... is that chap that sends a new tax code every year wishing you to work as hard as you can so, you can provide a good income for the fat cats who sit on those green settees, incidentally I might add, that this year I'll be 82 years young. I'll say no more about that! Fresh salmon was superb ant the roast beef likewise, the champagne bottle which was a special one, nine litres, was offered by my friend Dany, unfortunately he was unable to come. It was a beautiful day, friends mingle in the garden, the party finished quite late, the next day we were very busy with the clean up.

March 1989 My friend Dany from Italy paid me a visit, of course as I mentioned he was my best man at my wedding so it was a present by coming to see us again, he never came to England since that day. This time he came with his wife Maria, daughter Orietta and a very good friend of theirs the beautiful Giovanna, a wonderful lady. I was over the moon to make them sample my food at the restaurant, apart from that we took them to sightseeing the beauty of Kent, including the Dover Castle, Dany was very impressed to see such beauty. One evening after our dinner in my house we were discussing more or less our achievements in Switzerland, then Dany mentioned Princess Snowdrop, Giovanna said that she wanted to listen to the record, I played the record and translated the best I could the moral of the story, she loved it, and she mentioned that her husband produced quite a few Musical plays in their

(A scene from the Italian production)

ocal theatre, and she also said that; he will definitively produce it, if translate in Italian. Of course as it happens I already had the Italian version written down, she took the record and the script home and the musical tracks which were used on the original LP. Within two months Princess Snowdrop or shall I say; Principessa Bimbaneve that was the Italian title was premiere in Italy and run for two full weeks being in a small town that was good. I had to make my appearance the first evening, so I had to depart to Italy very quickly, unfortunately Edie could not come, but I couldn't tell you enough how good it was, the choreography

was first class, the kids performance was one hundred per cents great, you can't go wrong with kids, they can learn so much faster than the adults, the stage was decorated with real pine trees, I was absolutely flabbergasted a video was made so I could take the recording home and many photographs to show Edie, which I always remember she was in tears the first time she watched it, it was certainly a memorable experience. I will never forget the effort that my good friend Dany and his daughters did for that production, they spent hours and days rehearsing with the children, thank you all I shall never forget that.

Summer 1989 The restaurant fame was spreading in America. I think I mentioned this in my previous pages, never the less, Fromer's food guide which was published by Simon and Schuster, leading New York publishers, they made us really proud by saying; "The Ristorante al Porto in the region of Kent's England brings its continental flair for its food and outstanding atmosphere to many of our citizens and others visiting Dover and its taste by housing an Art Gallery, with the exhibits for sale. Thank you Fromer.

Business was as good as ever, but losing two waiters, wasn't what I wanted, in all the years I had the restaurant I must have changed no more than five waiters, and that is a record in catering business, so while I was looking for their replacements I carried on with part timers, I fouds girls were much better and more reliable, pity I couldn't have them full time. Tony my chef wasn't feeling very well, so he was off work for a couple of months, finding a chef was another problem. I tried so many times to employ a second chef but unfortunately everyone I employed was not up to the standard Tony required, mind you I would like to say that Tony was a bit jealous of his kingdom, perhaps he was afraid that someone else would take his job, chefs can be very difficult to deal with, and they are also very temperamental, in saying that.... I had to go in the kitchen myself with his son Lino as my assistant, he was only seventeen then but he was really very good, he was could almost a cook as good as his father, not as fast though, but with my help we managed to carry on beautifully. Later Tony was well enough to take over his job as before, but having had a rather complicated operation he had to take it easy, so I left his son with him who gave the support he really needed.

Summer 1991. Paul just turned twenty one. I thought he was old enough to decide for himself what he wanted to do. I knew he had already applied to join the Customs, but his first application was turned down, he was quite good in the restaurant business and I was hoping he would join me, but the decision was his, I asked and I told him the business was good but there were improvements to be made, if he wanted to follow the times and the trend, maybe I scared him on that presumption, and he knew that wasn't easy to run such business, for instance when Tony was sick I went through quite a difficult patch, as it wasn't easy to replace a chef like him, Tony was working as three people put together, but with a bit of perseverance we got over it.

Paul applied again to join the customs and this time he got the job. He seemed to like it a lot, of course I missed him in the restaurant as I had to employ someone else, although during weekends he came to help us out, but soon after he gave up the spaghetti business completely.

My son Peter turned seventeen and was still at school as he wanted to go to University. Weekend and school holidays he was working in the restaurant too. I asked him as well if he wanted to join the catering business, I thought that was a silly question, as he wanted to learn the computer technology. never the less he never refuse to help us out in his free time, he was getting paid for it, not a lot though, he used to tell me and he still does..... and so we had 1992 knocking on our door, with Paul in the Custom and Peter at University, both doing well.

(Me surrounded by my hobby)

February 1992. The restaurant business started to slow down a bit, January and February were the worst months, as people was recovering from their Christmas festivities expenses. So I thought to do something to keep myself active, started to write a story, I suppose I was thinking about some Arab country's wars, but it turned out to have a different title. I called it Love and Music, it was actually based on the middle east war, but without political inclination. I phoned Jeff my lyric writer from London and told him about my idea, he said he wouldn't mind to read it. I went up to London, we met for a drink and a sandwich and discussed it, he liked it but he was thinking of a different title, I thought why not, so I left him the script and the tape of the preliminary recorded songs, twenty two in all, quite a lot I thought, but that's me anyway... sometimes I go over the top. He phoned me back a few days later and said that the story was interesting and decided to call it "The crescent and the Cross" After all he concluded, beside being a war story is also a love saga between the daughter of a rich Arab Ambassador in London and a pop singer not so well off, few months later the project was completed, but I thought it was a bit too political, in fact that was the response from various interested parties and production companies, so it never got anywhere. I suggested to Jeff to change the plot with a lesser non political ideas, I even said that with all the terrorism going around the world we could be bombed by some crazy ideologists, no as usual he wouldn't have it, he thought his idea was great and it did not need any changes whatsoever he also told me that some of his friends said that was very good, mind you they all say that. Left it dormant on a shelf for years, and one day I decided to write the whole story as a book format with a different title; "Music the food of love" which is now published by Amazon. (More of this later)

Chapter 29
Our 25th wedding anniversary

I thought my problems were all solved, I was wrong. The highway Authority decided to renew the dual carriage way that takes the traffic to the docks, so in matter of a few days we were closed in, no cars were able to park anywhere near or quite far the restaurant, the works were supposed to last for a few months only, but unfortunately one of the diggers unearthed a Viking bronze boat ten feet below the road surface just outside my restaurant, so the works had to be halted and a team of archaeologists were called in to dig up the boat, what a mess. All the businesses along the road including mine were up in arms as we were all losing money, luckily in the end we were all compensated by the Government (I wouldn't have got that in my own country, I'm pleased to say) as a matter of fact I have a small car down in Italy and ten years ago the bank paid my road tax twice, they applied for a refund, sadly I am still awaiting for the money to be refunded, they disgust me they are a lot of takers, I said in first chapters that most of the Italian beside of some being nice people the rest they are all thieves. Nearly a year later the boat was unheated, restored and put in the local museum, soon after the road was opened to the traffic. History says; that the site where the restaurant was, it was sea claimed land, in fact the claimed land goes back into town five hundred yards or more. In my cellar the floor was made of pebbles from the beach. Few months later news came that Ron my publisher sadly passed away. I thought my musical hobby would die out too. Ron was a divorcee and had a daughter living in Poole, and when this happened she told me that she was no interested in his father's business. Ron had under his company name my songs copyrighted for twenty four years, that meant I was tight up with him for another tenyears. I contacted the PRS (Performing rights society) and asked their opinion, they suggested I should contact the   next of keen,   I rung Ron's daughter Enrica and asked her if she would sign back my copyrights, luckily she agreed without asking any payment, then the PRS gave a licence to be a music publisher and record producer. So, "Sanrocco Music" was born.

May 1992 We organized our 25th wedding anniversary really well, we invited all our friends and lots of our customers. Why not? They flipping deseverd it, as they kindly supported me with their money all these years, and we really wanted to show them our true friendship, good friends are not easy to find. Tony as usual made me proud for laying a superb amount of food display he kindly prepare, and Lina his wife Lina made a beautiful cake, called yhe grand mother gateau, we had that on the menu for many years, and it was the favourite of many of our regulars, all went well and very fast, like our 25 years of marriage.

(Happy 25th wedding Anniversary)

January 1994. Here we go again, I thought! Our company (AGM) Annual General Meeting. Everything went well, naturally for the first time we had a tough year, but there was no complaints, as we still made a little profit, perhaps I was the only one moaning, my partners they were smiling, probably thinking they I never had it so good, of course they never done a sodden thing so they had it better than I, I was telling them that I was getting a bit fed up, I could have been a bit run down, maybe the thought of my two boys not wanting to carry on in the business had something to do. In any case I suggested out of the blue, if anybody would make me an offer I would sale my shares, I wouldn't hesitate to semi retire, mind you I was nearly 56 then. Marco my partner, who was more or less the guide of us three, asked if i had any idea how much I was worth, should a buyer make an offer, or perhaps he suggested that he could make an offer, there and then I said I wouldn't know. But I probably would if sat down and do my summing up of properties and goodwill. I went home and have chat with Edie, naturally she told me that was entirely my decision, but she told me to make sure you not to give it away for nothing, further more she knew how shroud my partners were. So, I come with something that satisfied my thoughts and my figures, but on the other hand he might make me a better offer. Gone through my papers again to make sure that I wasn't leaving out something, or making any mistakes, but I came with the same total, I thought that was really great if they would accept that, my name was at least worth half of that price, in business like this the goodwill is worth quite a lot. The next day we met over a cup of coffee, and I put a tiny piece of paper before Marco' eyes, didn't take long to give me an answer by saying he agreed, of course he suggested with some conditions, such carrying on for another two years working as a consultant say for three days a week, this was not on the contract, as I would get paid as before, as to fade myself out of the business, so the regulars wouldn't notice or realize that I was leaving, however, it was a deal I couldn't refuse. I told Edie and she agreed, and she added that it was entirely my choice I told her that such offer would set me up financially okay. Right, few days later we went to a solicitor and he draw up an agreement, which we got a couple days later, and it wasn't long before we both put our signatures to the deal. I stared to work three days a week,   after six months Marco came to me and said that they were thinking to employ a new manager to run the restaurant, just to learn the ins and out of the business, I said that I was very pleased to work with a new manager, I told him to go ahead and as soon the manager will start I will finish, I didn't need to train anyone for that matter, if he was a good manager he wouldn't want me to tell him what to do, a week later Marco told me that the new manager will start the following Monday, so I made sure I took away what was mine such the paintings on the walls, which Marco didn't want to pay for them, he thought they belong to the restaurant, I said he was wrong they were private, anyway some of them belong to my supplier, he actually didn't know that I broke up with Giorgio, anyway it wasn't his concern, my last day I said goodbye to Tony and the boys, incidentally my son Peter carried on working there for another couple of months until he went back to the university.

Chapter 30
A sad end of a beautiful Restaurant

This new manager started to make many changes, starting from the menu. He was French so he completely made up up a new menu all written in French, can you imagine English people to go to an Italian restaurant and to find most of the dishes in French? In a matter of six months the business started to decline to almost zero, I was getting all the reports from Tony, I always remember Tony rung me at home one Sunday morning and he said to me that the previous evening they only had one customer all evening, I just couldn't believe that, thinking that each Saturday I was fully booked all year around, even during the winter months on a Saturday I was doing nearly one hundred customers, considering that I only had 14 tables, so on the weekend they had to be reused two or three times, that used to be my special day, because the takings of that day were enough to pay the weekly wages of all my staff. A month later the restaurant closed down, they put a notice on the door for refurbishing, that wasn't so, in the meantime they kept Tony doing breakfasts on their little hotel down at the docks. Three weeks later they reopen the restaurant with a new name "Valentino". I just could not believe it, after 25 years, it was like the world fell on me, I really felt like ringing Marco and say something, then I thought; why should I, I don't belong to that any longer, and really it doesn't concern me!

Valentino was opened and of course that French manager was still there. One day I went to visit Tony at his house and of course he was telling me practically the life story of this French chap, he was saying that he had a restaurant in Canterbury and in a matter of a short time he went bankrupt, too, quite unbelievable, fancy my partners employing a chap like that, I just couldn't believe it. Valentino was doing very bad, and one day I got a call from Marco, and asked me to stop by for a coffee, he wanted to ask me something. Over a coffee they ask me if I would come back to the restaurant, they were desperate to bring back the old regulars, I asked them; Which restaurant? He said Valentino, I just laughed, and asked him if that was a joke, he told me he really meant it, and said that their manager was prepare to work with me nicely. I told him that if he would get rid of that French chap, I might give it a thought but then I said that I would not come back to a restaurant with a different name, I also added that would made me a laughing stock in front of my regulars. Ristorante al Porto was a good name and a good restaurant that made a lot of money for all of us and you two ruined it by calling it Valentino, I simply told them that they had no idea what they done, I made them realized that by changing the name they simply would not get back the customers, and that was the end of our meeting. Few months later they went bust losing all their businesses for the sake of their incompetence, sorry mates but I thought your scholarships thought you a better way of running a business.

Having lost their all their businesses my ex partners disappear in thin air, could not understand why, to this day I haven't heard from either of them, I can't think what I've done to upset them that much, in fact I thought I done them a favour by selling my shares, if only they would have kept me on a consultant that wouldn't have happened, of course they were very sorry to have agreed on paying me that amount of money for three days work, equalled for a full week that I was getting when I was running the place. A lot of their employees have lost their jobs when the bailiffs shut down all their places. My good friend Francisco who was running the small hotel they had down the docks lost his job too, and some back wages they owed him, he was telling me, but when the bailiffs arrived an early morning to put the locks on, Francisco and some others they were thrown out on the road. He was a very good friend of mine indeed, we used to work together at the White Cliffs Hotel he was the one who introduced me to my ex partners. Yes, I did feel sorry for my good friend Francisco, good job he had a little two bedroom house in Dover so he had somewhere to go, few months later he decided to go back to Spain, and enjoy his retirement in the sun, he was born there, right in the south Estepona. He put his house up for sale, which I bought and wished him all the very best, we still keep in touch a few times a year, especially on Christmas time.

To try and forget all these misfortunate adventures, Edie and I decided to join a friend of ours, a nice Cornish chap married to a lovely English girl, they had two daughters, they run a pub in a small town here in Kent, and he's done well, I must say. His daughter wanted to get married in the Seychelles so he obliged, what some parents wouldn't do for their children! He invited a dozen people, some families some friends, and us too, but we paid our own way, and I was glad to do so, we had a nice holiday, two full weeks, cost me a bloody fortune, I can't imagine how much he cost him, as he paid for the whole lot, he was extremely generous with his guests, and most of them they were simply takers, never mind John you were a gentleman to everyone.

One day we booked a boat and went on this deserted Island, the boat people organized everything for the day including food and drinks. After we arrived they started a BQ with some beautiful fresh fish they had caught, everything was going well. As we were enjoying their delicious fish, and some cold beers, all of a sudden our picnic was disturbed by a nasty wind and the sky turned completely black and there we were told to rushed back to the boat as fast as we could, after five minutes on the boat we were struck by a terrible   thunderstorm, which got so nasty that the boat people could not control the wheel, however, it took us nearly an hour to dock on to the beach of the hotel, which usually would have taken us fifteen minutes, some of the girls were really seasick, and as for myself I don't want to hear about small boats and deserted islands for as long as I live, and furthermore I cannot even swim, I thought that was the end of our holiday.

August 1994 My entire first year, I felt a bit ungrounded, went to Italy three or four times, and of course I had my garden to look after, I loved my own salad, especially the red Veronsa and the Valeriana, that is lambs lettuce which grows all winter long, it's superb.

Chapter 31
My first record production

September 1994 Sometimes I asked myself if I made the right decision, I really missed my customers, and the money of course, but I thought I had to do something to forget my catering life, and one rainy day I called up my good friend Tony Martin the crooner, I just said to him; shall we make a CD? "I'd love to!" he replied. Tony Martin was a good guy, in fact sometimes he was even too generous, I greatly admired him, he was a real singer, with a voice almost like Frank Sinatra, and most of all he was a real professional, although he never got the right recognition that he deserved, of course there are some people they say is not good, and this kind of people think Rod Stewpot is better, if anything he's the luckiest performer, not the singer, in the world as he hasn't got any voice at all, never mind I would accept criticisms only on a such line like that for instance, he's not my kind of singer, then of course I would agree entirely, because not everyone have the same taste in music. However, we decided, as I finance it, but I said I would want five of own songs on it, he agreed and for the rest of the songs I left it up to him to choose the ones he wanted and the production was to be on my own label "Sanrocco Music" However, in the end we made a nice choice, all evergreen, including five of my own compositions. But I must admit with the new music revolution of the new generation, it was not the young people choice, but we had quite a successful radio plugging, not only in England but in Italy and in Spain, yes one of the major station played it quite a few times.

(The CD front cover of Tony E Martin)

SM001

SANROCCO MUSIC

The Unforgettable

Tony E. Martin

" Maybe

This

Time "

including five new songs

To start with he knew a musician called Dave, who also happens to be a first class arranger. We asked him to do all the arrangements, these were completed in a couple of weeks, and they were really first class. The recordings were done in a Rochester studio, when we saw this recording studio, it was almost like a shed, we looked at each other and I better not say what we were thinking, however, we were wrong but they wouldn't have been done better at the Abbey Road Studios in London. I must say it is a fantastic experience to see someone in a recording studio, the atmosphere is just out of this world, that is, if you like music and good singers. There we sat down and worked out the art work, the photo, history etc., The disc and cassettes were pressed in London, and a few weeks later we received the goods all boxed up. We were over the moon and very excited indeed.

(Tony signing his CD to a buyer)

The CD was launch with high distinction, the local newspapers were very generous and BBC local radio made us really proud. DJ and presenter Paul James even said that it was the best CD of the year. They were on sale in many shops in Kent, and we sold quite a few thousands I must say, I supposed if we had done a better marketing we would have sold more, that's one of the most important things, the marketing, and to be quite honest we were both little green on that subject, Tony sold quite a few during his gigs, I took them around to various shops, but that wasn't nough I was counting on him to make a success of one particular song of mine; "Mama, how can I forget your loving?" I remember a few months before, Tony performed this song in front of a few hundred people in a local hotel and believe me he received some outstanding ovations. I was there with my wife and Tony's wife, of course I was filming the whole performance, which is now on You Tube.

Tony was in the Royal Marines for many years, and also in that profession he was the main singer with their band. That was really a great orchestra they had, my wife and I went to quite a few of their concerts, one of which it was at the Royal Albert hall, where he sung a couple of evergreen numbers, we were treated like royalty as we were with Christine his wife, yes, we were given a box, which if we did not had to pay for, it would have cost us a fortune I'm sure. What an evening that was, at the end we went to a fabulous restaurant with some of his musicians mates. Few years later the Royal Marines were moved away from their barracks in Deal Kent, and some of them retired gracefully, that's when Tony and four of his friends they formed their own group called "Tony plus Tangent", and they were kind enough to play for my Princess Snowdrop LP. which was published a year later. After that my publisher and I thought to produce a single for Tony and his group, he sung two songs of mine on it, this was quite a success and was played on BBC radio2 quite a lot, it was distributed to a lot of records shops, one of which it was WH Smith in Canterbury, and four shops in London. I don't think you could do that now days, there aren't any shops left, I think the only one is the big HMV, even them I saw their records selling to near enough to nothing. Sad really the music industry has just fallen to pieces in the last few years, I don't really know what caused it, it is certainly a big blow for a lot of singers and musicians, myself I had something like fifty songs published but very rarely you see royalties coming through the door, well I think it was fantastic until it lasted, I must have written well over five hundred songs, I presume one of these days they'll end up in the old dust bin.... very sad!! We done Tony.... We didn't make a million out of it but we certainly had some great moments which will last in our hearts forever.

Chapter 32

An exciting retirement

July 1995. Paul and Tracey tighten the knot, they go married in a very old church in Dover, his friend Richard and his brother Peter were their best men. The reception was very smooth, this was followed by a reception in the local hall, organized by the in laws and ourselves, everything went as planned, the food was supplied by outside cateres and we supplied the wine, and I made sure there was plenty, leaving the bottles on he tables, sadly there was something missing and that was, as usual no one from my family side were present, that happened when Edie and I got married, so there again I was an Alien, I really felt like one believe me. Sometimes I ask myself, why do I have to feel like that? No matter how many years you are in another country, you will never be part of it completely, I suppose there's nothing to be ashamed of. So to make things worse this was followed by a Turkish honeymoon, naturally I would like them to have had an Italian one.

(Paul and Tracey married)

While the newlyweds were enjoying themselves amongst the Turkish crowd, I decided to take Edie, Christine, Tony and their young son Ben to Italy. I was there few months before visiting a few radio stations where they already had Tony's CD and of course they wanted to meet him, for various interviews, so we spent two lovely weeks in our place on the Lake Garda, and meeting Italian DJs and presenters, it was another special adventure, which we enjoyed tremendously. I went to say hello to the owners of the Grand Hotel where I spent my first years as a waiter, my lady boss wasn't there, her son was and the only son they had, he remembered me strait away, I gave him one my CD he was so pleased that he offered Tony if he would performed a few nights in the hotel, but unfortunately we were towards the end of our holiday, and that wish could not be granted. We were welcome by three independent radio stations where I was very acquainted with some of the DJs, no word of a lie, when the CD was on air, the engineers and staff were clapping Tony, that's how much ovation he received. We recorded three shows of half an hour each which they were broadcast each day for three days. We were all over the moon, mind you Tony drunk so much that I had to get extra coffee to wake him up in the morning, I am sure he would have been very successful if he had performed at the Grand Hotel.

We kept the last few days for relaxing time and visiting more places that even I have never seen and of course we were waiting to see the article in the Brescia National newspaper, for Tony was quite an achievement, just out of the blue in an Italian national news for just a simple CD, not so much of that simple, it very important as it contained five

We never stop sapling the local food, we often talk about the restaurant who had over fifty starters, and you had to help yourself as much as you fill your tummy, the end was approaching fast and before we knew it we were on the plane and back to the same routine, we had a lovely holiday, in the company of lovely friends and guests.

March 1997. A little part time job came along, I really didn't want to work, as I did enjoy doing nothing, but since life was getting a bit boring I accepted. The local; police had ask me if I wanted to be a translator for the Magistrate Courts, that if they caught any bad Italian people doing something wrong. So I came in action in front of the Magistrate, they did paid me well, but they didn't catch many naughty Italians.

November 1997. We went up to London to watch Peter's award ceremony, which was held at the Barbican centre. He passed his BSC (Hon) with full marks. It was certainly an exciting day, not only for us but also for other parents, you could see the joy on their faces. Soon after he found a good job for himself with a pharmaceutical company. It was a well earned position. We were extremely happy.

May 1998. A phone call came from Italy, it was from a local school in the town where I was born, they asked me if I could provide the material of Princess Snowdrop, the funny thing they wanted the English version and not the Italian, they already had the LP and children involved they knew more or less the songs. Coincidence that I had planned to go down myself, as I had to do a few things to my place and then I could see my sister. The following week I went down, met the teacher who was going to produce it, very charming lady, she was in fact the daughter of friends of my family, we met and discussed, she was telling me that she could do it in three weeks time, but I told her that I could not stay that long, but some member of my family would attend and some friends perhaps. However, as they already knew a few songs, she asked me if I could go to the school next day, as the children they were performing a couple of songs just for me, which they learned from the record. The performance of them kids made me very emotional, at the end I was more than delighted, I thank everyone and wish them good luck for their forthcoming performance. I heard it was very successful, although they only done it for two evenings.

During my last week in Italy I decided to change a car, I had an old banger in the garage, an old Renault, and I kept having problems. A friend of mine told that the Italian government had a scheme, which if you had a car older than ten years, you could exchanged it in any selling garages for a new one getting a discount for nearly two thousand pounds, provided the one you bought was new. My old banger was 14 years old, I had no problems, so I bought a nice Fiat 500 I called it the jewel in my garage, it was beautiful cheap to run, and easy to park, I did enjoy my short trips to my friends and really I never had any troubles what so ever. Years later we sold our property, as we didn't used it as we shouldhave done, I kept my lovely Fiat for another two years, as my niece had parking space, but then I sold that too, I regretted that ever since, because now if I go to Italy I have to hire a car, which it does create problems with insurances when you get old.

Well and relaxed I was back in Dover, and not so surprised I was, to see my old restaurant still with locks on and grass growing out of the old windows, them silly baggers of my partners , should have listened to me, and for certain they wouldn't have ended up like that. Few months later I noticed some bulldozers knocking down the three buildings which we owned. it was thought that they were going to build some apartments and shop, as the old buildings used to be, but sadly that land is now a lonely car park, I suppose these parking owners are making more money than doing anything else.

Chapter 33
Welcome to our first grand daughter

September 1999. After a short illness my good friend and chef Tony passed way, it was sad and a tremendous loss for his lovely wife Lina and his children Angelo, Michael, Lino Enrico and Maria. A wonderful family of hard workers. In spite of this we are glad that they are all doing fine. We visit each other quite often, we also have the casual dinner together, this pleases us enormously and makes me feel proud that I've always treated them with respect, and almost making them part of the family.

October 1999. We were holidaying in Italy when a telephone call came from Elizabeth, Mike McKenzie's wife. Unfortunately it was very sad news, Mike died in Spain Estepona, in their holiday home. He was seventy seven years old, I was told that he loved so much Estepona and there he wanted tio be buried. Few months later Elizabeth phoned me from London, inviting us to a thanks giving in memory of Mike to held at St. Pauls Church (The actors Church) in Covent Garden London. Edie couldn't come but I made sure that I was there.

There were quite a few big show business names including David Soul whom I met on other occasions, he sung a special song dedicated to Mike, as they made a film together called "The stick up"I was quite disappointed that there was no mention of our Musical "Princess Snowdrop" which we wrote together, after all it was truly published and recorded on LP record, he always was so proud of it to have been a partner of our precious Children Musical. This was followed by a get together at the Connaught Rooms in the Strand. I did not go as I was not invited. Never the less, it was an honour to have known Mike and work with him in many of our compositions, his kindness gave me the will to achieve many true dreams.

June 2000. We went to Italy for three weeks as we were invited to a wedding, we thought at the same time to have a nice holiday. We spent the first week on the beaches of Lake Garda, as the weather is always perfect in tyhe month of June. I guess we were out every evening dining with our friends, we had so many. They really like to make you feel at home. Naturally we try to do the same when they come to visit us in England. Our friends wedding was out of this world but very exhausting. We were pleased to get back to England as we were all excited about the arrival of our first granddaughter, in a way we were a bit worried as our daughter in law had a very difficult pregnancy during which she had to take it easy all the way.

July 26 2000 To compensate the sad loss of two good friends of mine my son Paul and Tracey gave us our very first granddaughter called Lauren, it was a very welcome and a very happy news. A beautiful present from mother nature and father nature too.

(Tracey, Paul and little Lauren)

Few weeks later, doctors founds some complications, maybe caused during the birth. Spent a week in a special Hospital in Lewisham where she was kept under observation. Paul and Tracey stayed there too and the four grandparents in and out worrying. After a week she was discharged, free of anything, surely we were glad to come home.

February 2002 It was our first trip on the Eurostar, we went to Paris, John and I thought to give a treat to our girls for Valentine's day. It was a bit cold but the train was very comfortable. Got there okay, we stayed at a Motel through a taxi recommendation, it wasn't too bad, the worst thing was ... a bit far away from the centre, but it worked out alright. Before anything else we made a booking at the Moulin Rouge for the next evening, that was easy enough, then we went to a good restaurant, a bit expensive but it was first class. John suggested that I should pay the bill and he would leave the tip, I said; "we go fifty/fifty and you leave a tip as well clever glug." We were really looking forward to see this famous Moulin Rouge, we were all dressed up like an evening at the queen's ball, black suit, black bow tie, two lovely young girls...... and the rest, but when we sat at our table, we noticed that we were the only ones dressed up in such a manner, in fact people next to us were wearing jeans and tea shirts. The dinner was terrible, we probably enjoyed more if we had eaten in McDonald, at least we were compensated with a good show. I don't remember but I'm sure we didn't leave a tip. We spent the next day visiting some more places, we came home early the next day. finishing the trip with a nice steak at the local pub. At least that little adventure gave me an idea to right a show, probably better than the Moulin Rouge itself. Finally, I must say John behaved himself for a change, that made our Valentine excursion fantastic.

Chapter 34

Another baby on the way

July 2003. We had a wonderful visit from three Italians young ladies, good friends of ours, Thank God they only stayed the weekend, They sure used up all our energies and theirs, Kathia the one on the right, next the old fellow, Tatiana maybe trying to kiss me, an old acquaintance and looking young as eve, then there's the beautiful Monica always there to tell us something with a smile, actually she

really smile and looked like Meryl Streep, all three were fabulous and a very good company, I don't think my budget could afford again to take you out to a restaurant. you did cost me a fortune, OOPS... sorry about that I didn't mean it really, it was my greatest pleasure, even my next door neighbour was impressed, with you three as he was kind enough to taxi them to the airport. I told his wife not to worry he was safe. However, we had a wonderful time, we took around Kent, and they were very impressed with the Kentish regional the pubs, but most of all they loved the Canterbury Cathedral, of course that is something not to be missed when you visitthat beautiful town, that's where they insisted to take this photograph, I really felt a bit shy, My wife was the photographer, I think she done a good job indeed. What a weekend that was!!

September 2003 Paul, Tracey, little Lauren and the two of us, went to Italy by car, especially for Lauren she had a chance to meet all her relatives. We had a terrific time, the weather was still very summery, we were on the Lake nearly every days, but the most memorable day was down at he farm of some friends of mine, Lina and Barabba, what a guy is this Barabba he took us around in one of his coaches and horses, all over he fields and many charming villages, it was e very exciting experience, in fact his horses and coaches are used in films and at the Arena in Verona when they do the Operas many times, , he showed us many photographs where he starred in them. The day before we left, we went to this restaurant, the chap who runs it, is a mate of mine, it was getting a bit late, we went in, we actually were starving, we spent all day long on the Lake with just a few sandwiches, I said to my friend Gino, let's not waste any time just bring us four steaks a pasta for the girl, some salad, plenty chips bottle of wine and some soft drinks..... No problems, he said, two minutes later he came back and he told me quietly that he only had horse steaks, I told him to bring them, these lot wouldn't know the difference, between beef of horse steak! The meal ended with four cleaned plates, and Tracey said to Paul; "You know Paul I was so hungry I could have eaten a horse" (that was of course the old English saying) Paul replied to her; "You just did!" She looked at him for a minute and said; "What's the difference, I really enjoyed, actually I could have another one!" We all laughed, thinking that nobody knew, but Paul understood alright!

November 2003 Tracey announced that she was expecting, it was a complete surprise, as they never thought she would have another baby, not according the complications she had with Lauren.

May 2004 Amy was born, yes, Lauren had a sister, and we think she was made in Italy, if our Lauren is 24 carat gold, Amy is most certainly a true star.

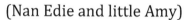

(Nan Edie and little Amy)

It was certainly a surprise event, since we thought that would never happened, there you are our treasures. Totally different from one another, Lauren has dark hair and Amy is blond, they are both beautiful and very lively, and very cheeky. Lauren has started school and she seems very clever with her learning. What else can grand parents say? nothing more really, we said everything!!

Well, well...That was a surprise, I understand they met in a London bar, one cold November evening, how long ago, I don't really know, my young Peter is not the sort of chap that tells me everything, as most of the times I have to guess it, and so my darling wife tells me the same. In 2005 Peter was having drinks with some of his university mates and Shirley was doing the same with some of her colleagues from work. They chat away, exchanged emails, they are very lucky now days, in my times we couldn't even exchange phone numbers as we didn't have one, I remember well, when Edie and I met, we could only contact each other from a telephone box outside her house, no she wasn't waiting outside the box for the phone to ring all day long, I used to tell the time I would ring her then she'll wait outside the box.....Oh never mind, it's too complicated for you youngsters. Anyway, After a month chatting away on their marvellous technology, a few weeks later he made her welcome in his bachelor pad and took her around the coast for sightseeing. Alternatively she made him welcome in her beautiful house in Sidcup for Christmas Lunch, although we missed him that day but we didn't mind. Did we? I don't know so much! I gather from that point a true

(Peter and his delightful wife Shirley)

relationship started, few years later they decided to go to New York to see some friends of hers, that was well planned, but not perfect, as he ask for his birth certificate, maybe that's what you needed to get married in New York , to cut a long story short, they tighten the knot there and then, without telling us. very naughty, I'd say, in my times I would or we would never have done a thing like that, only famous people were allowed do that. Never the less, Edie and I were not very happy, to think that we were not present to their important day, they did made us feel second best.... we might be old fashioned on these matters but we believe that families are important in such moments as these, after all in life we only have a mother and a father, and we will not be around forever. And of course, one day they will be old too.

June 2006 Edie and I were in Italy for a short break, when one afternoon I had a phone call from the major of my town, asking me if I could spear five minutes of my time to go and see him. We met in his Council office, and there and then he told that they were producing and publishing a book of various autobiographies from local people who in their time had achieved some popularity or done something unusual. H e added that as I have been in England more than fifty years, he knew more or less what I had achieved in all that time, and also he heard some of my popularity from a few of my school mates, so he offered to include me in this book, my autobiography at no costs to me. Most certainly I accepted, and to be honest I was overwhelmed. I came back to England and drafted, a dozen pages of my history as a short synopsis and sent it to my friend the Mayor personally. Few months later I went to Italy with my wife as I was told that the book was published, Edie was with me when I was presented with a couple of copies, and to our surprise we were invited to a theatrical evening in a large Restaurant, as some of the stories were revive on stage, it was like a Sun and Lumiere type performances, accompanied with wine and food of that era. It was and unforgettable evening which we'll never forget.

Chapter 35
My seventy's birthday

May 2008. So.....I have reached seventy, thank God I still have with me some good memories, it's very sad for some people or I should say some of my friends , they lost theirs in the clouds and like magic they'll never remember them. Will it happen to me one day? I hope not. In the meantime I decided that on my birthday this year, like any other, I would take my family out to a superb restaurant, mind you not an

(Seventy? I nearly forgot I've gone through that)

expensive one, but good one I hope, I'm sure there must something out there to satisfy my taste and pocket. Just the six of us, isn't that wonderful, I thought. My wife agree for a change, but my son Peter said he couldn't come, as he had somewhere else to go with Shirley his girl friend I guess with some other friends, maybe friends are more important than parents. Is this the new generation? Well, if it is, it is a very sad one. I wasn't very pleased as usual, but I thought it can't be helped, then it was just the four of us, my son Paul, Tracey, Edie and I. Well, some kind of celebration on your seventy, I said to myself. However it was decided, mind you, in the end it wasn't my decision where to go, it was my wife's.... it's got to be the Moonflower, she loves Chinese, maybe she should have married one...I thought! The Moonflower a very elegant, but it was much smarter when that old Mexican mate of mine was running it, he was a good front man, of course having worked for me in the past, I think he was copying my style a little bit, forgive me for saying that.

The booking was for seven thirty, and funny enough we got there in time, knowing that Paul and Tracey are always late, in fact they were waiting outside as we arrived, the waitress said we were to sit upstairs, I said why can't we sit downstairs as the place seems empty. Edie said .. no, the table was booked upstairs, I thought so be it, I'm going to foot the bill anyway. Up we went and a chanting of happy birthday sounded out from a large corner table, where friends of our were greeting me like a hero, for a moment I thought it was a dream, but it's nice to be treated like that once in seventy years. Oh, I felt quite safe , as most of my friends are in the police force, not that I know they caught any robbers or criminals in their life, they will confirm this if they are going to write their own autobiography.

The food was excellent and the wine was flowing, I made sure that no one had to beg for it, or having half glass only, it seems to be the fashion in England, I remember once I was at a dinner party, I was there with an empty glass for twenty minutes, I then ask my host, where should I put the empty glass? He replied; take to the kitchen sink! So that was the end of the wine ration. The dinner ended with a fabulous birthday cake, with my ugly face on it. Our guests were really wonderful, I hope they will forgive me for making a few silly jokes. We missed many others friends who live faraway; the lovely Christine and Jacques, Max and Margaret and many Italians including my sister. A special thank you to my sweetheart for paying the bill, I'm sure she had to save up hard for that.

September 2008 Amy started school... she was very excited as she said she wants to learn fast, so she'll be able to read some stories to her Nan. At the same time Lauren started the big school, where I come from we call them the elementary. we were not wrong to think they would do well, so far I can say they really done very well.

Beautiful September, as usual that month has been always the favourite to spend a few weeks down in Italy in our sweet pad and as usual we asked some of our friends to join us. Edie does enjoy their company so she can practice her English a bit more, so to speak, so do I for that matter. then I don't have to translate so much, but in saying that, some of our Italian friends speak English. When we go down to Italy we just can't keep up with their invitations, their dinner parties are quite exceptional. However, a week later we were there, Dave his wife Pauline, Jean and Terry, join us for a week, Oh, I forgot Dave brought his dog, he did ask us first, lovely one too, nearly as big as a lion.

The same day they arrived, we had a phone call from Franca, asking us if we were free for dinner. I told her that we had some English friends arrived, so we could not accept, with no hesitation she said bring them along the more the merrier, so the six of us joined her party with nearly twenty people. Now I felt very sorry, because only their daughter speaks English and she wasn't there, so I had to translate the whole evening. It was a good party, the food was excellent, so was the wine. Next day we took them to visit the Lake Garda which they enjoyed tremendously. Few days later they went to visit Venice, we stayed at home dog-sitting and prepare the dinner for the evening, we thought to invite some of our Italian friends. I remember we had more than fifteen people that evening, and our friends seemed to be more acquainted with the Italian language, we did enjoy the evening between long chats and some hilarious jokes, Dave was sitting next to me and I was telling him that after fifty years in England I still feel an outsider, although inside me I feel more to be English than some English born, I would never say bad things about England, but sometime people make me feel like an Alien. It was then that Dave suggested that I should write my autobiography on that subject, so here it is Dave, I have decided I shall call it "I was an Alien" and I hope you will enjoy it, mind you it wasn't easy as I had to researched my vast collection of photos, half way I found it quite easy, because you don't need much imagination to put things down that happened in the past.

December 2008 Christmas arrived quite quickly, and I think we had a little snow, not on Christmas day, but around that time, and that was the best time for Edie and I to get the Christmas tree ready, Edie and I really loved to enjoy the festivities with our two granddaughters, it seems unnatural that when we get old we tend to enjoy more the grandchildren than our own children, could it be because our children once they have grown up they start to forget that particular loving feeling that parents miss so much, or maybe they have other things in their mind, like new friends, yes I think sometimes they probably have more feelings for other than us.

That's our favourite photo, and to see them opening their present it was just a present for us, nothing could

replace that in a lifetime. I personally was very attached to my parents, I thought the world of my mum and dad, presents..... all I got it was a plate with a few oranges and some dry nuts. And I only wished they told me more about my ancestors, but sadly, I suppose being just after the war they didn't have much time to tell us stories as they to struggle so much to earn that slice of bread, you can imagine if they thought of telling me about my ancestors.

So, as January 2009 was knocking at the door, Edie and I were already thinking what to do in spring. But in the meantime we had to organize the Christmas festivities with a few dinner parties with the families and with some of our friends. New year became quite important, exchanging house parties, yes, we done this in turn. Few years ago we used to go to celebrate in style, but that became to expensive and a bit boring and for the fact that we had to hire the transport, never the less, that was nice, and so we were waiting for the snow falls that once upon time we used to get, but it seem the weather has changed so much that we haven't seen a bit of snow for years. So with the company of the old fire place and the television and a few glasses of wine we were saying bye, bye to the winter and welcome to more hours of daylight.

Chapter 36
Goodbye to our second nest

March 2009 Yes... Spring is here......Edie and I decided to put our Italian apartment up for sale, we had that for over 35 years, and to be honest we did not use it as we should have done, and naturally if it's not being used it is going to deteriorate, and of course the up keep would become more, and more expensive year after year. We found that the Italian estate agents are not so good like the English ones, so we took it off their hands, and in no time at all we sold it ourselves. So the flat was gone, although with a satisfactory price, we know we would miss it, we would miss our Italian friends a lot with their evening superb dinners like no others can do, of course no comparison to the English ones ,if you can forgive me for saying that, if you don't believe me you can always ask my few English friends which they were invited too every time they visited us in Italy, and no matter what, we shall miss their beautiful massive markets, which we always looked forward to go and see, and buy a few things, not that we did buy a lot, but they are undoubtedly the best markets we have ever see around the world. Yes, we presume that we won't go to Italy as we used to, but luckily enough we found this small Motel, which is owned by some friends of mine and is fantastic. Their food and their accommodation is the very best, it used to cost us more to live in our flat than to stay in that Motel.

Yes, I thought I include a photo of my family it would be unfair not too, especially my parents they'll be always first, family were different then, especially Italians are very family orientated, sadly now   days the new generation I would say, I don't think they have the same feelings or loving attachments. Yes, the photo goodness me that was taken at my sister wedding in 1950, quite a long time ago, as I'm writing my sister is the only survivor of them lot and if you don't mind me too, as I am the very first on the left, next to my father and my mother, which I still miss them so much, my mother she would be 123 this year **(2020)** and my father would be 121, he fought for Italy on the first world war at the age of 16. My dear sister Irma 90 this year, is at present in a care home, after suffering two strokes, luckily she hasn't lost her memory neither her speech and I'm happy to say she's well looked after, and of course she was cleared of the present coronavirus19 that infected almost the whole world, England like Italy lost a lot of people and it seems to be an endless epidemic, God knows when the world will resume its normality, we are scared, and lots of people have lost their jobs, through business closing down, we are still in locked down, meaning we are very restricted to go anywhere, I sincerely hope I am wrong, but some world governments are hiding something from us, we just don't know the real cause, but I believe the truth will come out soon and will cause more problems for our society. Personally, I think that some experiment of some kind went wrong and this has poisoned the air as this pandemic has reached every corner of our planet. .

May 2014. Due to the crisis which eroded the whole of European Community, especially the Italian Government which had to make big cuts in their economy by closing the most important services to the Italian people not only in Italy but also in every other country. In England they to close almost all their consulates, leaving three of them, London, Liverpool and Bristol. Unfortunately at that time my passport was due for renewal and sadly it took me for months, to get an appointment, they required my fingerprints, can you imagine at 76 years of age all they wanted my fingerprints, I reckon they had in their files at least a dozen of my fingerprint, but let me correct myself; they probably lost them because they are a bunch of disorganized cretins, you have more imbeciles people running Italy than anywhere else, and we pretend to be a nation of conquistadors, little do you know what happened to the last one, well, I will tell you once again, he was shot and hanged upside down in a Milan square as the second world war ended, it is sad really to have to say such things about a country which I was born in. One point I must make though, Italian people don't like to pay taxes, and that has been going on for a long time, and now the government charges taxes left right and centre even the TV licence they pay it on the electricity bill, very clever I'd say! I became so frustrated with such bureaucracy, I've seen so many unfair treatments to my family during my life time, that I thought... enough is enough, as much I've always been proud to be Italian, but there's a limit to everything, so I decided to apply for citizenship, at least if I become British I shall my passport in a couple of weeks, I simply thought that there would be no problems, I' ve got a clean record with the law, in fact I never had even a traffic fine. Furthermore I've been married with a British girl for over fifty years, my two boys are British, incidentally, my granddaughter applied for her passport and within a week it arrived safely at her address, what a service, I thought if I was British I would say; "I am proud to be British" So by applying for citizen- ship I thought maybe one day I'll be able to say that.

June 2014 I filled up my application of 70 pages which I downloaded from the internet, giving away every possible details of my life, my family, my parents (which they would be at that date120 years old if alive) plus the sum of £906 in advance, which I thought a real daylight robbery, what the hell, all my family are British, so why not joining them? And that of course I would not be called

bloody foreigner by some clever git. The rules on the application were very clear, which they said; That it would take six months to receive a reply and if I would not be accepted I would lose my fee. Obviously I thought because they got feed some fat cats lazy bas...... good for nothing, not unlike myself which in 60 years I have never took a penny from the state, I paid my taxes and I still paying them as I write this, employed people in my business, done a lot of charities and many others things, except of course I never gave blood, but I thought about that in the past. So the application went with my cheque, and the Home Office duly reply, and said thank you for your application and thank yuou for the cheque, I thought that was very nice and very polite. Seven and half months went by and I was still waiting to hear from the Home Office, I thought, their were getting worse than my lot. I was starting to get very edgy, so I phoned up and ask them what was happening to my application, the lady I spoke to took my case number and said I would receive a letter in the next few days. (that's the time when ladies started to take over the running of the country and drink a lot of Chardonnay. Nothing happened for two weeks so I phoned up again, and another lady said the letter was in the post. (See? Chardonnay are taking over again) Quite true! I received a letter the next few days asking me to fill up another application. I asked them why several times, they just repeated themselves saying that I had to fill up another application, so I asked them if they had lost my first application, they kept saying that I I have to fill up another application or (Finally they said) you will lose your fee, if you don't do that. I never filled up another application, as I thought it was wrong and unlawful for not admitting that they had lost my application. I wrote a long letter and told them that I did not want to become a British citizen in my coffin, therefore I would not fill up another application They replied without saying anything about my comments by they included a cheque for £80 by saying that I did not need to pass my test for the English language. So am I a British subject or am I not? No... I guess I am not, so I will stay as I am, it means that I have been subsidising some holiday's fat cat or my money has been used to pay the bill for some big colossal wedding recently, they should be ashamed to spend such amount, when there are still so much poverty here and everywhere else. I just cannot understand the mentality of some people. Have I have been wrong to be an honest fellow?

"So I have a suggestion on this matter pay attention citizens"

Wouldn't it be better if any immigrants having settled and worked in this country for a number of years, having paid its taxes, further more with a clean record and wouldn't it be an honest law to give them a choice to get a Citizenship should anyone wish to do so? Instead to dish out Citizenships to any Tom, Dick and Harry provided they pay good money. I think the actual law to get Citizenship is preposterous, and very unfair especially to someone like me; A tax payer for 60 years, married to a British girl, my boys are British... So what's wrong with you people? Yes!! That goes to say that after all that England is better than my own country, this is why I wanted to become a citizen, but unfortunately I got stay as I am......AN ITALIAN ALIEN!!

Chapter 37

My new venture

January 2015. So be it! What's the use of worrying about silly things like that? If I don't do something else to take my mind off of what supposed to be right, now it's all gone wrong.

A few years ago I wrote a story which at the same time I adapted as a musical, it took me six months on and off to write it, taking oin consideration all the cooking I do in my kitchen for my family, but I managed okay to complete it. **"Love and Champagne"** the title, with some twenty five songs all originals, performing time two hours long. It wasn't an easy job , I can tell you that. I managed to recorded on two CDs with the generous help of my devoted friends.

(The book front cover of "Love and Champagne)

It was great fun, we were fifteen of us, and it took us two whole Sundays, and both them days I made sure that refreshments were available followed by lunch and plenty wine. The result was very satisfactory, considering I am not a professional arranger, but my lovely Roland Keyboard done the job quite perfectly. Love and Champagne is a love story set in the 1930sh of an Irish immigrant trying to make his fortune in London, after struggling with all sort of jobs he finally gets one where he can make some money. Having gained that, he managed to transformed an old pub, like a music hall, with music dancers etc., Love, music and a bit of sex is unavoidable, and the old jealousy is not missing either, with the main character's girl, which she's in love with a barrow boy, this girl turns out to be the daughter of the now rich immigrant, who's had an affair with her mother when he was lodging in her parent's house. The end is very touchy and a very happy one. So that was done and polished, but none of the local operatic societies wanted to do it, as it too much of a challenge. So my good friend Rosemary, told me to write as a book format, because it is a lovely story, I did and thanks to Amazon, it is now published. Thank you Rose for your suggestions. I really did appreciate them.

I thought "Love and Champagne" was easy enough, so I started a new story, this one was called; (And it still called)**"The lonely, lonely clown"** The plot is very intrigue, with a bit of a trilling story, set in the 1950sh. It's the story of an old Rumania family who ancestors after ancestor run a Circus, they settled in the north of Italy many, many years ago, of course they have been through great wars but with their dedication they always survived and also over the years getting themselves well-known, their main celebrity was always the clown, they knew well that making people laugh was the best thing to make them forget their troubles, but we all know clowns are always very lonely, that's why I call this love story "The lonely, lonely clown"

(The front cover of "The lonely, lonely clown")

Although they struggle during the second world war, they were left happily in business thanks to their friend Fritz an high SS German Commander who became friendly with Romano the Circus' owne. The Circus became quite famous after the war, thanks to young Tatiana a beautiful Ukrainian acrobat. But after a few years Fritz turns up as a theatrical agent. Fritz is a fantasist and a big liar, a drug supplier and a lover too. The Interpol is after him believing for having double identity. All this is unbeknown to his friend Romano from the Romanoff Circus, so Fritz is welcomed as usual. There's one murder well planned, which no one of the characters will never know who done it, except the readers of course. The plot is quite interesting as many others good and bad things happens to the Circus and to poor old Fritz. But it ends with a beautiful wedding of Tatiana and Cocco, Romano's son, everyone joins in for the happy celebration I thank you that this one too, is also published by Amazon.

After I went through The Crescent and the Cross and see the changes from my own original story Love and Music I realized how politically bad that was, no wonder a couple of producers rejected the show completely for that reason, so I carefully thought that I should do something to revive it, more than that I turned it to my original version, with a few changes and the title "The crescent and the cross" might as well be forgotten, which I've already mentioned its problems on page 107. The changes Jeff made in the story, sounded quite offensive, there's enough racism in the world, no need to create anymore.

(The front book cover of "Music the food of love")

GIULIANO LAFFRANCHI

MUSIC The Food of Love

* A fictional love story *

"Although from different countries, Robby and Shakira fall in love with each other and fight against a tyrant and oppression as her country is invaded by greedy neighbours.

So I thought of a new title and I decided I would call it; **"Music the food of love"** Yes, that fitted perfectly because is the story of pop singer Robby and Shakira daughter of an Arab Ambassador residing in London, their country is being invaded and a war breaks out with his neighbours, father and daughter go back to restore peace. Robby being a reservist joins the Allies and joins Shakira. Apart from a few dead people. The invaders are squashed, everything returns to normality. Robby, Shakira and the father returns to London safely. Shakira's father still believe in his religiously ways but he has no choice to let his daughter marry Robby, which they live happily ever after.

Not long ago my wonderful girls friends from Italy (I don't really mean girls friends as a love relations) Yes... they paid us a visit one glorious weekend and after that unforgettable visit they sent me this picture below, which as time went by they gave me an idea of a story, more than a simple story it is really a crime and a thriller one, and naturally it turned out to be my very best and my.........

(First book front cover of Julian's Angels")

.........favourite,. The first one you probably can guess that the title is; **"Julian's Angels"** starring three beautiful girls Natasha Nicole and Sofia, freshly awarded by the Scotland Yard Academy CID investigators, their jobs is to clear up a small seaside town from the drugs traffickers from European countries and gangs of hungry of protection money.

The girls meet Jools a restaurant owner who has to pay some protection racket to be able top run his business, he starts believing that those girls are his angels as they appear things start to change for the better. there are three consecutive murders, which are meticulous well planned, and nobody can find the murderer. However a lot of excitement happens including sex. With four convictions and a surprised wedding at the end of Natasha and Nat, one of Jools' sons, making a very happy ending. the newlyweds depart to their honeymoon to Venice and of course that doesn't seem to be the end because there's a sequel which is going to be more exciting and sexy.

"Julian's Angels 2" This sequel of the first one is is here to make you run for fear, it starts off with Natasha and Nat's honeymoon in Venice. They are staying in this luxurious Hotel, where within the first few days two dead people are found, but who's the murderer?

(The book front cover of; Julian's Angels 2)

The Italian Investigation squad has no idea, considering that the first one happened next to their bedroom's corridor as the body is found in a cupboard and the second is discovered two days later in a downstairs ladies toilette. During their staying Natasha meets police Inspector Rubbio, Natasha can smell some mafia connection and Nat finds a very interesting clues as on his last day of vacation walks around the market, needless to say their hotel is owned by the mafia. Back from their honeymoon more excitement happens as Natasha is now in charge at the Port of all the crossings operations. More drug traffickers are caught which helps to wipe out a London gang. It ends with the three girls getting a gold medal of appreciation each for their good work to enforce the law, plus Nicole and Sofia fall in love with two local boys. Again apart from some nasty discoveries about old Rupert thieving again, and some happy findings for Rupert's wife Jill, naturally ex lover John William the lawyer shows up, making sure to recoup what was lost in the past, enjoying both in full their loving weekends. It all ends well. My sincere thanks to Amazon for publishing this one too.

And "I was an Alien" this is the last for the moment. I'd say a very particular, it is my autobiography, moaning to people the things I have achieved, these of course they might not be as many and perhaps not very interesting to many people, but in all they gave me a lot of satisfaction..... yes.... I am proud of myself to show that I haven't been idle like some I know, yes there are quite a few lazy ones about, thinking that their luck will fall from the sky, but it doesn't work like that, I believe you have to have dedication and good will to get somewhere.

Giuliano Laffranchi

** I was an Alien **

A True Autobiographical Story
Of An Italian Immigrant

You might ask yourself, how come an Italian becomes an Alien?
Simple really, when you realize you are in another country
and you find people's mentality is so different, and then?
then of course is to carry on as an Italian Alien.
Can that be changed? Naturally, with money!

Here it is not so much a front cover but the inside can tell you some interesting things.

Chapter 38
Old age I decided, it's a gift

May 2020.....I am now, probably for the first time in my life, the person I have always wanted to be. Oh, not my body! I sometime despair over it, the wrinkles, the baggy eyes, and those white eye brows. Quite often I am taken back that old person that lives in the mirror (Who looks like my mother, whom I love very much) But I don't agonize over those things for long. I would never trade my amazing friends, (Although sometime I think: Do I have any?) I would say I enjoyed my wonderful life, my loving family, for less grey hair, just appearing, or for more money, I wouldn't say no to that. As I have aged, I've become more kind to myself and less critical of myself, I have become my own friend.

I don't chide myself for eating that extra slice of salami, or Parma Ham or indeed some Parmesan, not to mention for not washing dishes, (I reckon I was born to that mainly) Or for buying something that I didn't need. I am entitle to a treat, to be messy or extravagant. I have seen too many dear friends leave this world too soon, or become unfortunate enough to lose that good sense that mother nature gave us at birth and of course to understand the great freedom that comes with ageing.

Whose business is it if I choose to read, play my keyboard, or play on the computer until four am and sleep until noon? I will dance with myself to those wonderful tunes of the 50, 60, and 70. And if choose at the same time, to wish to weep or think over a lost love....I bloody well will! I will walk the beach in a swim suit and I will dive into the waves (Even if I can't swim, I'll stay in the shallow water) Despite the pitying glances from the jet sety. They too, will get old one day, if they are lucky! I know I am sometime forgetful, but there again, some of life is just as well be forgotten. And remember the most important things.

Sure over the years my heart has been broken, how can your heart not break when you lose a loved one, or when a child suffers, or even when somebody's beloved pet gets his by a car? Broken hearts are what give us strength, understanding and compassion. A heart never broken is pristine and sterile, therefore will never know the joy of being imperfect.

As you get older, it is easier to be positive. You care less about what people think, although some of my so called friends still take the piss out of my accent, or indeed if I make a single mistake on my verbal English, yes, it does hurt sometimes, mind you, when I think some of them they don't even know their own language or how to spell properly, so really, I don't want to question their ignorance, because I know they are. So to answer your question; Is this the main moral of my Autobiography? Yes it is, because I've earn the right to be wrong, I know far too many people who never believe to be wrong, and that is sad!

To cheer me up I thought I finally introduce you to my lovely family, as you can see they are all laughing, I think we must have been out to a restaurant and probably I got stuck with the bill that's the reason they are all happy.

(My lovely family, Mum, Peter, Paul and myself)

I can honestly say that 2020 hasn't started all that well, first the terrible pandemic which hasn't yet ended and now to make it worse we are now having the racism big problem, of course the worse is actually in the US, blacks against whites, it is a sad situation, but of course this happens also between white people from different countries so it is everywhere. So, to end my saga I'd like to mention just few of the many incidents that happened to me over my good years in England.

1) **In** the seventies I was coming back by car from an Italian holiday with my wife and three years old Paul, I was stop Customs, so I did declare some goods which I bought in Italy, all that was done and paid for, then the officer dealing with it, decided to have a second look in the boot, and naturally I had SIX bottles of liqueurs in a box, which incidentally I did not buy as they were given me by my brother as a present, these I did not declare, and the officer was really nasty, he took my car to pieces and I was held in a room for three hours asking me all sorts of

questions, I was really treated like a criminal for six bottles of liqueurs I was in tears, and in the car I had my wife and baby Paul with measles. in the end he gave me two choices; to appear in court and face jail or pay the fine of ONE hundred pounds. I told him I wouldn't have mind to appear in court to object about the treatment I got, as I said that, I vividly remember this officer looking at me and laughing, I don't remember the exact words but that what he said; "What treatment are you talking about? Don't you forget that you are a foreigner in our country and you have to obey our laws, you only had to declare the six bottles, and by not doing so you tried to evade our law!" I explained to him and apologized but he wouldn't hear of it and as we lived in Cornwall it was too far for me to come to court in Dover. The officer told me it wasn't his problem. almost six weeks wages amount for six bottles of liqueurs which in any case they were not stolen. Luckily I had a cheque book with me and I paid the fine, that officer was definitively racist, not only against any skin's colour, but a true racist against anyone coming from outside his country. I will never forget his shit face for as long as I live, this is how hate and racism starts.

2) **I** was delivering some clothes to my wife's little shop, so I had to park on one yellow line, as I was unloading a police car stopped and told me I shouldn't park there, I said I was delivering for the shop, he said okay, but as he heard my accent, he probably thought "Another bloody foreigner" and so he said that I should switch off the engine when I don't drive. I told him that the engine was switched off as I showed him I had the car keys in my hand, I knew at that moment he felt embarrassed and to cover his embarrassment he said that he saw the fumes coming out of my exhaust pipe. I found that funny and I just laughed, that really upset him, and he still said that next time he would

fine me for not respecting the code, but I told him he should have more respect for honest people. He went in his car without saying a word, I guessed what he was saying to his mate in the car; "bloody Foreigner" (Maybe something nastier, which I dare not say) That is racism! Or call it what you like!

3) **I** think during my humble life I have been kind, most of the time I'd say, I do not recall to have been nasty or offended anyone or fell out, unless of course someone had forced me, which is quite usual now days, as people seems to fall out very easy, probably because comes a time when you realize that some people, perhaps without knowing,takes you for granted or taking advantages of your kindness. This brings me to a small episode which I can't get out of my mind. It was a lovely summer day, my sister arrived from Italy, with her companion, to celebrate her visit I gave a garden party, with good food and plenty wine, I borrowed a marquee bigenough for twenty people. The party took off wonderfully, with laughs and long chats, when all of a sudden an unexpected strong wing arrived which caused to undo the attachments of the marquee sides, as I was tighten those up I said; "This is typically English weather" In no time at all one of my guests remarked; "If you don't like it piss off to your country" Well... I really thought that was quite a racist remark, we all know that this particular piss head chap he's an idiot, as for his intelligence he cannot even write a proper letter, it is a fact that someone else has to do it for him. I could have told him to piss off too, but I didn't because I am smarter than him and also I did not want to spoil my party, I told Edie the next day, she was furious, she certainly would have given him a piece of her mouth. Naturally this twit is no longer welcome

in our house, furthermore he's not even a man enough to apologize, and believe me I met quite a few like him. I wonder why have those kind of breed. If anyone would ask me what was the worst hateful moment in my life, which I still resent and I will for as long as I live. Yes, it was that fine of One Hundred Pounds, because that was my first contact with a racist.

4) **W**hen we moved in our new house, I was trying to clear up some rubbish in my garden along the bushes and cutting their long edges, when all of a sudden I noticed a large bag full of tools, by the look of them I thought they belong to some plumber, and thought right away how bad that poor plumber might feel who mislaid it or got it nicked. I showed to my wife and of course we both agreed that I should take it to the police, so I did, the officer in charge, thanked me and gave me a receipt, and told me that if the bag was not claimed by three months or so, they would return it to me, as I was the finder. Past the set time I went to the police showed him the receipt, he looked on his book and told me that the bag was not claimed, and he said I could have it there and then, he told me to wait five minutes while he went to the lost property's room, sadly he came back and said that the bag was not there, he apologized and asked me my phone number as he would make enquiries about the where about and let me know, to this time, I am still awaiting for that phone call. I was telling this story to a policeman friend of mine, and he suggested that I should have written a letter to the chief Inspector, quite honestly I didn't bother as I don't know anything about plumbing.... That's what I call a good abiding law honesty!!

All this has set me free, maybe a little grumpier, I like the person I have become, I'm not going to live forever, but while I am still here, I will not waste time lamenting what could have been, or worrying about what will be, And I shall drink a glass of wine every single day to wish good health to my good friends.

And so I have reached the end of my little story, and as I recall with great sadness, I mentioned at the end of my short introduction the nasty problem we are facing at the moment and that is that Corona Virus which it still amongst us, and God knows when life will return to its normal phase. No one seems to able to give us an answer how exactly it started, so many stories has been said. So what next?   I think I shall leave the future to my children, grand children and all the rest, in the meantime I'll better leave you and do something else as I guess someone's looking for me.

"Goodness me, they won't leave me alone, why are they are looking for me? Never mind I put up with them all this time I   suppose I can put with them a little longer.....See you later folks!!

A thought from the Author

      I always thought that only famous people write autobiographies, actually let me correct myself, they don't do it, they have other people writing them, and really, that it's not the same thing writing it yourself, what you know and comes out of your personal brains, cannot be the same when you tell stories about your personal life to someone else. Yes, my life as you have read it was not so simple, neither that famous in fact when someone has to depend on another country to improve your knowledge or getting a proper job, especially if you start in a country where everything is so different, from the language to the innovative or shall I say introduce new ideas, with a mentality of your own, it hasn't been an easy task. Things I did, like writing songs and trying to sing them, writing stories, I know for a fact that some friends and my own family they might think they are all rubbish, but I don't give a toss, I know I did enjoy doing them, at least I haven't hurt anyone's feelings, all I have to say is thank you.

Giuliano Laffranchi

Index

©I was an Alien

Words approx: 58,650

Drawings by the author

Notes:

"The Ristorante al Porto" in no longer trading

"The old Coach House" is no longer trading

Printed in Poland
by Amazon Fulfillment
Poland Sp. z o.o., Wrocław

62300083R00112